SPeak Performance

SPeak Performance

*Using the Power of Metaphors
to Communicate Vision,
Motivate People, and Lead Your
Organization to Success*

Jim Walz

First published in 2014 by
Business Expert Press, LLC
222 East 46th Street, New York, NY 10017
www.businessexpertpress.com

ISBN-13: 978-1-60649-890-3 (paperback)
ISBN-13: 978-1-60649-891-0 (e-book)

Business Expert Press Corporate Communication Collection

Collection ISSN: 2156-8162 (print)
Collection ISSN: 2156-8170 (electronic)

Cover and interior design by Exeter Premedia Services Private Ltd., Chennai, India

First edition: 2014

10 9 8 7 6 5 4 3 2 1

Printed in the United States of America.

Abstract

Every leader needs to move people to action and align everyone's actions toward the same goal. But how is this best accomplished? Words are a leader's greatest tool, and metaphors are the most potent combination of words available. If a leader wants to be successful in communicating vision, motivating people, and transforming an organization, he or she must understand the power of metaphors and learn how to use them well. Through the proper use of metaphors, anyone can become a better leader, align his or her team with their organizational values, and lead the organization to success. Metaphors can activate vision and mission statements, enliven goals and objectives, and literally align every aspect of an organization in its intended direction. In *SPeak Performance: Using the Power of Metaphors to Communicate Vision, Motivate People, and Lead Your Organization to Success*, Jim Walz, PhD, shares his proprietary method of developing metaphors for use by any leader of people. The knowledge gained from the principles in this book will help leaders develop stronger vision and mission statements that are action oriented, and it will provide a schematic to organize goals and objectives that are relevant and focused on accomplishing the vision. Organizations can be transformed in the way they do business and find the ability to compete in a global marketplace more effectively than ever before. Whether you are an aspiring leader, a supervisor, manager, or corporate executive, this book will provide you with communication tools that will take your leadership to the next level and beyond.

Keywords

leadership, management, organizational change, management communication, business, strategy, organizational behavior, communication skills, leading, organizing, organizational development, systems, processes, vision, mission, motivation, motivating, success, successful, business management, entrepreneur, entrepreneurship, organizational culture

Contents

Part 6   Structural Mapping

Part 7   Bouncing Back: 15–Love, and Back in the Game

Acknowledgments

This book has been a labor of love, and I want to thank Jeff Shelstad, President, Business Expert Press, and Rob Zwettler, Executive Acquisitions Editor, for their faith in this project. I also wish to express my appreciation to William "Bill" Denzel for his expert representation, continued encouragement, and editorial expertise. My thanks go out to Glenn Burris, Ivan Misner, Charles Lee, Jason Womack, Paul Robere, Kimberli Lewis, Rogers Hellman, Robert Mottice, Michael Louis, Ilene Bezjian, Craig Lawrence, Erin Mellinger, and Dan Lucero for their kind words and encouragement along the way. I also appreciate Jim and Lori Adams, Terry and Gayle Samples, and Pat and Mindy Crowder for being there when I just needed my best friends around me. To all my past MBA students, we traveled the world together, and the friendships we built will never be forgotten. To Mom and Dad, thanks for taking me in and giving me a life, and to Mom and Dad Thompson, thanks for your love and support. For Jamie and Lindsey, I hope you always go after your dreams and never settle for second best, and know that I'm your biggest fan. Finally, to my most vocal cheerleader, lifetime partner, and wonderful wife, Laurie, you have always been there for me, and I'm a better man because of you.

Introduction

If you've ever tried to instill a sense of vision and mission in the hearts and minds of the people in your organization, you know that this is a challenging task, to say the least. Even if you are successful at communicating the vision and mission, maintaining your strategy and achieving them can be extremely difficult at best. It is because of this that I developed the process of *metaformation*, the activity of developing, mining, and applying metaphors to motivate and transform leaders and organizations. Metaphors have the power to activate vision and mission statements. They can flow down through goals and objectives and align every aspect of an organization in the direction it needs it to go.

Metaformation is accomplished by

1. using attributes to structure metaphors, which is *metaframing*;
2. identifying the elements of a metaphor, which is *metamining* (deconstruction);
3. combining these elements to build new metaphors, which is *metaforming* (reconstruction and innovation); and
4. applying these new metaphors to transform the way we lead organizations, which is *metaplying* (application).

By following the principles and processes in this book, you will find yourself and your organization discovering a new voice—one that is interesting, inspiring, and motivating. It will move you to new levels of leadership. It will bring a transforming message to your organization and get it back on track. You will begin to SPeak Performance in everything you say and do.

Without underestimating the importance of trust, character, and vision, *communication* is your primary tool, whether you are a leader in business, education, the church, government, the military, entertainment, or any other field. When others are looking to you for leadership, knowing what to say and how to say it is the secret to success. We all need leaders who can communicate vision, mission, and strategy effectively, and keep our organizations motivated to carry out their missions. Keeping all the pieces of an organization aligned and heading in the right direction is difficult, but it's the primary task of a leader. Leaders who can do this properly are in short supply. In every field, competition is fierce, and the noise in the marketplace causes so much confusion that an organization can easily wake up one day to find itself so off track that it's almost impossible to get back. A case in point is the demise of the once super record store chain, Tower Records. In 2006, Tower Records closed down its U.S. chain of stores, and although still operating overseas and online, it is no longer the primary source for today's youth to buy records.

Tower's founder, Russ Solomon, remembers opening his first store in San Francisco in 1968. "These kids that came in on a weekly basis to go to the Fillmore or Avalon or just experience the Haight [Ashbury] scene or the whole scene," Solomon told NPR in 2006. "They wanted to know where music came from. They wanted to know the roots of all the music that was being created here by those bands." Russ Crupnick, who analyzes music retail for a firm called NPD, adds, "Tower was an icon. It was a magnet. It was Disneyland the first time I went in there. But later Tower just sort of lost relevancy." Big-box stores undercut Tower in pricing CDs. Baby boomers stopped buying new music. Young people stopped caring about liner notes and owning a physical product. Crupnick notes that, by the late 1990s, Tower Records was no longer a music lover's mecca. It was just a higher-end Sam Goody (a mass-market music retail chain found in malls across America). "They became very ordinary, in terms of their expansion plans," Crupnick says. "And arguably, as they went to about 90 stores, they lost that whole idea of being special."[1]

This has been the way of so many organizations in recent years. Companies such as Bombay, CompUSA, Lehman Brothers, Washington Mutual, and many others may have experienced a better ending if they had employed a process to ensure they stayed on the right path.

The Power of Metaphors

By nature, I am a storyteller. I find the stories I love the best are about real people. I love to read about their life experiences and the people and situations that have impacted their lives in such profound ways that they were able to see deep meaning in these experiences. Often, in my reading I envision metaphors that help me to understand what these people have learned from their life experiences. In this book, I introduce the story of a business leader named Jason—a fictional (and somewhat autobiograph-ical) character—that I hope you'll find entertaining. But the point of the story is not just to entertain you. The story is a vehicle to communicate a new approach to starting, rebuilding, or redirecting an organization through the application of metaphors.

A metaphor is a thing regarded as representative or symbolic of some-thing else. It's an implied comparison between two unlike things that actually have something in common. When I considered the value that metaphors have in providing insight into my personal everyday actions and reactions, I also discovered the power that metaphors produce, which can activate and sustain action while transforming our organizations.

As you read through each chapter, you will see me use two types of phrases: similes and metaphors. Although they are related, there is a sig-nificant difference. Similes are the weaker phrase. "Life *is like* a box of chocolates," is a simile. Similes typically incorporate the words "like" or "as," drawing a side-by-side comparison. Something is as good, as bad, as dark, or as light, as the other thing. Metaphors, on the other hand, are stronger. "Life *is* a box of chocolates" is a metaphor. Metaphors typically use "is" without the comparative qualifier "like," effectively stating that the two things being compared are more than comparable; they are the same thing. The reality is, however, that the things are not necessarily interchangeable. Unless it is spelled out, the metaphor leaves it up to the reader to find the elements that make them the same. Even though there are some structural differences, for the purposes of this book I treat metaphors and similes the same. You will see in those instances where I use a metaphor as an example, the strength and commitment that the metaphor creates are much more effective than the simile.

The original Greek meaning of metaphor is "to carry something across" or to "transfer" something. One example of a metaphor is, "Humor is the shock absorber of life; it helps us take the blows" (Peggy Noonan, *What I Saw at the Revolution*, 1990). Peggy alludes to the way that humor takes the bump out of life's bumpy roads like shock absorbers do in cars. Another metaphor is, "If a man does not keep pace with his companions, perhaps it is because he hears a different drummer" (Henry David Thoreau, *Walden*, 1854). Here, Thoreau compares the pace of walking through life to the drum beat of a drummer, suggesting that some walk at a different pace than others. A final example comes from John F. Kennedy: "The energy, the faith, the devotion which we bring to this endeavor will light our country and all who serve it—and the glow from that fire can truly light the world" (Inaugural Address, 1961). President Kennedy compared energy, faith, and devotion to light and implied that they have the same illuminating impact on the world. Metaphors such as these help us to gain a deeper appreciation for who their originators were and what they saw as important in life. As in President Kennedy's example, a metaphor has the ability to move an organization to action.

Life Is a Performance

Along with being a storyteller, I am also a lover of music and theater and everything that goes with them. I am a musician and majored in drama and theater in college and have been on some type of stage for as far back as I can remember. These stages were not always theatrical stages but stages of life where I played a role surrounded by others playing their roles. In my early years as an actor I would listen to directors trying to bring out my best performance by using metaphors to describe what they wanted from me. In playing a medieval king, I might hear, "Be like a lion, grand and majestic." If the director was looking for more joy and laughter, he might say, "You have just won a $100 million dollar lottery! That's the kind of joy and glee that I need from you!" I soon discovered that metaphors helped me, not only on the entertainment stage but also on the stage of life. As Shakespeare famously described,

> All the world's a stage,
> And all the men and women merely players;
> They have their exits and their entrances,
> And one man in his time plays many parts,
> His acts being seven ages.

Metaphors can affect who we become and what we do with our lives. The act of "becoming" can be a passive act or a deliberate act. I can allow life to yank me around or I can take action to become someone that I aspire to become. Depending on how we apply them, metaphors can help us describe that preferable future or take action toward it. I'll go into this in subsequent chapters.

For the purposes of this book I chose to use three metaphors that most readers can relate to, in order to describe how transforming principles emerge through their application. These are playing cards, driving fast cars, and balls. I used the metaphors in the descriptive process as they have applied to my life, while illustrating their transformative nature through the story of a fictional artist management and record company.

In the following pages I introduce the metaphor that "life is a game of cards." Naturally, life is much more complex. But card games and life have many similarities. They both involve rules, strategies, interventions, alliances, and good fortune. Whether one's card playing experience is from the perspective of poker or fish, most of the basic principles such as the value of each card, the sequence played, and the aggregate value of a hand are consistent. I realize that in some circles a game of cards may be considered a game of chance and not acceptable by certain moral standards. I respect that, but life can seem like a game of chance at times, so the act of playing cards is an appropriate metaphor.

I also talk about the metaphor of driving a fast car. This is a distinct joy for many people and a horrible necessity for others. As you know, driving requires a significant amount of attention. One must be attuned to how best to operate the car (or truck, if you are a truck type of person). Either way, driving requires that you steer clear of obstructions, react properly to avoid collisions, and navigate a route in order to reach your destination. Driving can sometimes seem competitive, such as when other cars try to cut you off, or you speed up to get to the exit ramp. Traveling through life can be like driving a car, and success or failure depends on how we handle the driving experience.

Finally, I discuss the metaphor of a tennis ball. I do this in the context of the music business and show how metaphors can transform an organization—in this case, a record label. Balls are meant for throwing, hitting, kicking, or passing. They follow a trajectory that begins with the initial impact that drives them forward. The distance and arc of the trajectory is dependent upon several things, such as what the ball is made of, how much energy is behind the initial launch, and how it reacts when it hits a wall or other potential stopping force. Each of these elements of the metaphor can be applied to how we fly through life and how we deal with interruptions.

Throughout the book I use analogies and call them metaphors. Metaphors are one type of analogy. You may also encounter several other metaphors in the book, beyond the three just mentioned, that are used to describe certain situations. These are included mainly because they best capture what I am reflecting on at that moment.

It is not my intent to represent that the use of metaphors is the *only* way to describe a life or transform an organization, but it is a powerful one that is not well understood and not always effectively used. My hope is that my story will encourage you in some way and provide you with a new tool—a strategy to use metaphors to describe your situation, develop your leadership effectiveness, and transform your organization. Metaphors can help establish successful behavior patterns, and in the larger context, they can be used to assist leaders as they work to inspire and motivate their workforce and map out strategies that will breathe new life into their organizations. Now, let me begin by using a metaphor that will weave itself throughout my personal story.

Beginnings

We all come into life in the same way; we are born of a mother and a father. Not all of us know their names or have any connection to them other than sharing the same gene pool. But one thing we can know for sure is that the moment of birth is the moment that we each begin to walk down a path that will have its ups and downs, triumphs and defeats, and joys and sorrows. Like a game of cards, some begin this trip at great disadvantage, having been dealt useless cards, while some have a guarantee of winning because of the advantages their cards bring. We don't get to choose this; we have to play the hand that we've been dealt. That, however, doesn't mean that if we've been dealt a crummy hand we are guaranteed to lose. On the contrary, a crummy hand can be just the thing we need to position us for a great victory.

Nineteen fifty-four was an odd year for some. Although a cease-fire arrangement between the United States and North Korea had been signed a year earlier, isolated conflicts flared up along the DMZ. Soldiers, airmen, and sailors were still being sent into harm's way, and some were still dying. Partly to show a continued presence to the North Koreans, but mainly to provide support to the Japanese, post-World War II occupation of Japan by the United States was in full swing. U.S. and Japanese government agencies and private industry worked feverishly to rebuild a war-torn nation. Anger, animosity, and shame were masked by energy devoted to healing broken hearts and broken lives on both sides. In the midst of this, many children were born of mixed race, to Asian and Caucasian couples: some married, most unmarried. These children, for the most part, were dealt crummy hands.

Their faces reminded everyone of the horrible anguish that was experienced on both sides of the Pacific-Asia war. Their existence, born out of love and lust between two people, symbolized the subservience of a conquered nation. They were a reminder of the shame felt by many Japanese over their defeat by the Allied forces. They were Japanese, yet they were not. They spoke the language of a defeated nation, but were not accepted by that nation. In many respects, they were children without a nation. Stories are told about the not so discreet abandonment— and sometimes murder—of these children. They were dealt crummy hands.

If you know the Japanese, you would be horrified and unwilling to accept that a people who some would say represent the epitome of grace and dignity could act in this way. I would agree with you. However, unless we walked in their shoes during this very difficult and humbling time, we should refrain from casting the first stone.

I was born in Japan that year, the odd year that all these things were happening. I was one of those children born of love and lust between a couple, one of Asian descent and another of Caucasian descent. I was dealt a crummy hand. To top this off, I contracted polio shortly after birth. I was most certainly dealt a crummy hand.

At this point, you might be feeling sympathetic toward my situation. On the other hand, you might be thinking, "Hey, I was dealt a crummy hand, too! What makes yours more crummy than mine?" Well, my point is not to compare hands but to share a story (using metaphors) that can help you become more effective as a leader and transform your organization in the process.

Although this book is written from a man's perspective, it's not necessarily meant to be directed toward men only. Some of you ladies have been dealt crummy hands as well. In some cases, the disadvantages that you faced growing up surpass those of most men. This story is applicable for you as well, and the use and benefit of metaphors can help male and female leaders alike.

When I was contemplating whether to write this book, I reflected on the fact that so many people—literally millions around the world—are currently out of work, living in poverty and squalor, wondering where their next meal will come from. Many have lost their homes, their personal savings, and their hope. If this is you, be encouraged.

You may have been dealt a crummy hand, but as you read the chapters ahead, you will see that—regardless of how bad your hand is—you can win the round. And, if you persevere, you can win the entire pot. As you move through each chapter, you will begin to see metaphors in your mind that describe your own life. Jot these down. You can discover what you were meant to become. By understanding how metaphors provide insight, and finding ways to apply new metaphors, you can achieve your dreams and the success that you were destined for in life. Then, take that knowledge into your organization and transform it by applying new metaphors. Become the leader that you've always wanted to become. Your curtain call can be a glorious one!

PART 1

Metaformation in Action

CHAPTER 1

Is This the Last Race?

Movin' down the back streets
Pass the speed of light
Sparks burn inside me
Gas and air adjusted right
Layin' down some rubber
Needle's in the red
—(Street Lethal, Racer X, 1986)

For a long time, things had been going well with the business. As record labels go, it had pretty much hit the top of the charts and stayed there. However, in recent months it looked as if it had begun a slide that could prove difficult to recover from. As the CEO, Jason should have seen what was happening. But for some reason he missed all the signals. Sony had recently closed a plant and laid off 300 workers in New Jersey due to what they called, "the challenge facing the physical media industry." They were referring to the introduction of iPods, MP3 players, LimeWire, and other forms of technology that had replaced the CD.

Jason guessed the first indicator he should have noticed was in the area of distribution. His company had enjoyed many years of preferred service and product placement. They had always treated their distributors well and with good terms; however, they were getting pressure from the marketplace as well as from their competitors. He started noticing their products positioned lower on shelves, and they were not getting end cap displays like they had in the past. Something was definitely up. Their online sales were also starting to suffer.

Their artists' numbers were dropping. They had less than 20% of their artists in the Top 100 Billboard rankings in all genres. This had never been the case. The road managers were complaining about the crowds at live events. They had thinned out, and greyed quite a bit. That was always a challenge. As fans get older, music does not hold as dominant a place in their lives as it used to. They buy fewer albums, download fewer individual tunes, and attend fewer concerts.

The label had to find ways to reach these audiences better, or they would have to let some of their older artists go. This was a tough call because it also involved the catalog of songs that they held publishing rights to. If they let the artists go, they didn't have a strategy to continue promoting the licensing of their songs. When their artists were working, other artists were still recording their songs. It was a dilemma that they had never faced. One bright spot was in the licensing of their songs for films and videos. However, this would not last forever as many new companies had sprung up to produce generic music just for that purpose. These were not hit songs but good background pads and mood audio.

Jason had also received a complaint from one of their top artists. They were threatening to leave because of the treatment they were receiving from their managers who worked for the label. Some of the older managers were getting a bit gruff when they worked with the artists. It was as if the managers were becoming grumpy old men. Most were still under 50, but Jason thought the business was starting to wear on them.

Managing and promoting artists can sometimes seem like babysitting. Many artists are very insecure and compensate for that insecurity by acting like prima donnas. Oddly, this happens more with the older artists than the younger ones. You would think that after the artists reach a certain level of success, they would find some security in having made it. But, apparently, the pressure of staying on top drives them to greater levels of insecurity. Jason figured this was one reason he had not continued as an artist. He could see the writing on the wall facing so many of his musician friends. He knew the better place would be in the business of music: helping artists, building an organization, and eventually growing old sitting on the beach.

As he walked around the office, he noticed that most of his employees were doing something other than working. Some were playing video games, some were on their cell phones, others were just sitting around texting their friends and family. Could they really be so dysfunctional that the empire he had built was now beginning to crumble around him?

Jason decided to call a meeting of the Executive Team. This included himself, and all the Vice Presidents. They represented A&R (artists and repertoire), Promotions, Publicity, Publishing Sales, Distribution, Ancillary Products, New Media, Television, Film, Marketing, Legal, Label Liaison, Business Affairs, Art, and Artist Development. He also invited the head of Human Resources, who, though not a "C" level staff member, he thought they would be critical to the conversation.

Jason called the meeting with just two days' notice and was met with a cacophony of rebuttals. Miles, from Sales, was heading to New York to visit his parents. Karen, from the Art Department, had a gift certificate and reservations to receive a full treatment at a local spa. And George, the Business Affairs guy, was headed to Alaska to go salmon fishing. Others were simply apathetic and treated the scheduling of his meeting with a lackadaisical attitude. Somewhere along the line he had taken his hands off the steering wheel and lost control of this once beautiful Porsche GT3 RS that had torn up the roads of the entertainment industry. They had been at this for a long time, and it was starting to show.

Jason had started in music many years earlier. He had been a musician, albeit not a very successful one. He played at the clubs as most aspiring musicians do. Sometimes he went on tour and lived in the back of a van or in some seedy hotel room that he shared with several other musicians. Most of the time he handled the business of the group because no one wanted to do the job. In time, he met a number of successful musicians, and it got around that he understood the business of music and had some creative ideas. Before long, he found himself representing several pretty successful artists. He also discovered that working with a partner helped to manage the growing stable that he was attracting.

Dillon, Jason's partner, was a great guy. He had been a successful musician in the early 1970s but had gone into the business end of things because it offered greater stability. Jason and Dillon hit it off right away. They would meet regularly at a local Irish pub and sit in a booth near the back dreaming about the "what ifs." One interesting thing that attracted them to this particular pub was the fact that they had a telephone in each booth. This was long before cell phones. They gave out the phone number of their regular booth to clients and business people who were able to contact them there most anytime of the day. They discussed the idea of a music management company and what it might look like. How would the company grow? What would they offer their artists? The answers would emerge in the months and years ahead.

A Powerful Metaphor

Jason had always loved how words were able to paint pictures. As an actor, words are the lifeblood of the stage. For a musician, words tell the stories and the music sets the tone and keeps the pacing. He lived with a metaphor on his tongue, ready to use it whenever he was trying to capture something complex and bring that complexity into simpler terms that were understandable and easily digestible. While he dreamed out loud, he began to picture in his mind, a beautiful new Porsche speeding down the Pacific Coast Highway, sunroof open, with Robin Trower blasting "Day of the Eagle" at full volume. He could see the future beginning to open up before them like the straightaway coming out of turn 11, in front of the stands at Laguna Seca where drivers can reach speeds in excess of 200 miles per hour. It was an incredible feeling to catch a vision that was so much in line with his love for music, his recent discovery of business acumen, and his desire to build something enduring. Jason was in the pole position and heading into the first turn.

Those early days revolved around casting a vision and establishing a foundation. His company had a vision to be the premier record label on the West Coast. Some of their friends were saying, "Music? Everyone in music is heading to Nashville. That's where you need to be." However, Nashville seemed too small a town with too little networking possibilities. Anyway, the artists they knew were far from Nashville and lived here on the West Coast. Because of his love for fast cars, the company's vision was characterized by the idea of sleek, fast, and exotic. Their vision statement was, "To be an international force in music that will change the lives of everyone who hears or sees the incredible mix of sound or visual performance by our artists and productions." They did not want to become just another record label. They were looking to conquer giants.

They developed a mission statement that gave them direction. And even though the road might take sweeping turns in the future, they had their hands on the wheel with enough rubber on the road to lean into the turns and navigate the course aggressively with complete abandon. Their team was firing on all cylinders.

Hard, Fast, and in Love with the Business!

Very quickly, their stable of artists grew. They were successful booking them into lounges, clubs, showrooms, and concert halls, which drew more artists. As their artist roster increased they were given more booking opportunities with venues around the city. Since they could find work for their musicians, the musicians began looking to them for recording help and promotional support. Naturally, they jumped at this and began signing them to recording contracts.

They vertically integrated and set up a recording studio with state of the art recording equipment. They negotiated agreements with Rack Jobbers to place their artists' products at eye level and on end caps. They contracted graphic designers to assist with album and CD jacket designs. Remember, this was all before digital recordings and the Internet. There was no such thing as downloading music. They brought in costume designers, famous hairstylists, and choreographers to help prepare their artists for live performances. They were becoming a full service record label.

In time, they established themselves as a fast, slick, and honest contender for the flag. Their engine was finely tuned and their drivers were rested and prepared to go the distance. Soon they were approached to provide soundtracks for movies, voiceover artists, and arranging services. Anything related to sound—they could do and were doing. At one point it became apparent that if they wanted to race in the Grand Prix of entertainment, they would need to shift lanes, and get into producing television and movies. And that's what they did in the following years.

After years of crossing the finish line ahead of the pack, it seemed like their pistons were misfiring. Their timing was off, and they were losing artists and deals. There were new competitors on the track who were contending for the pole position. Their musicians were getting older and they were not attracting artists like they had in the past. Their attention span was diverted from the road ahead, and their vehicles were breaking down under the strain. Finally, their pit crews were out of shape and lacked the motivation to turn good times in the pits. Overall, their company would come to a screeching halt unless they found a new metaphor to work with.

Their previous metaphor involved fast cars, hot women, and young drivers with the coordination and chutzpah needed to take on all comers. They were aggressive in their negotiations, brutal in their demands of themselves, and they looked out for each other. They were a team that was well synchronized and understood how each of them helped navigate the business. They had roles that were well defined, but no one ever complained when they had to lend a hand in another department to meet customer demands. They worked together, played together, and found their love for this business together. But that was then.

A Moment of Reckoning

As each of Jason's department heads strolled into the conference room that overlooked the city, he could see weary expressions on their faces. They knew something was up but didn't seem to have the energy to do anything about it. Recently, they had experienced some heated arguments that revolved around turf, budgets, and priorities. This meeting would be different. Jason needed to get his hands back on the steering wheel, feel the road beneath him, and start navigating the course again.

For a change, he took the floor immediately. In recent years he had allowed some bad habits to develop, which predisposed others to treat these meetings rather casually. His first bad habit was in delegating the running of these meetings to his Chief Operating Officer (COO). She was a good leader but was more of a tactician than one who could inspire others. He had initially thought, *At this stage of the growth of the company, who needed inspiring?* These were all professionals with degrees from top universities and considerable experience. He felt they needed better management and less leadership. However, in recent days, he discovered that he had been wrong. He knew that habits involved a routine that started with a cue. The cue, in this case, was his COO opening the meeting by welcoming everyone. It was usually rather dry and business-like. This caused the routine part of the habit loop to kick in. Most of his team would roll their eyes, yawn, or leaf through their papers. Today, he would open with energy, fire, and questions. He noticed that three of his main

Vice Presidents were absent. He didn't have time to deal with that now but would have to address it with them later.

Jason began by going around the conference room and asking everyone to give him things they thought had changed since they first came to work for the organization. This caught everyone off guard. They sat up, listened, and mentally prepared a response. One said the fire had gone out in the boiler. Another confessed that he had been approached by competitors with job offers but couldn't get himself to abandon ship. Another said that she felt the ship had lost its rudder. Each of these and the others gave him their thoughts in metaphors. The Human Resources Director confessed that the opinions expressed were widely held among many of the employees as well. Jason realized that because most of the Executive Team had been artists at one time, and that all of them worked with artists, they expressed themselves in metaphors like most people would carry on daily conversations. They were used to being around people who painted images with their words, which gave their words more impact. Based on what he heard, Jason realized they needed to change their current metaphor.

He went around the room and asked each of them to give him an adjective or phrase that best described what they were sensing about the organization. The table below lists their responses:

Current attributes
Lethargic
Unfocused
Too big
Not motivating
No more joy
Bureaucratic
Indecisive
Bound up
Too safe

He thanked everyone for coming to the meeting on such short notice and dismissed them to go back to their offices and play Angry Birds or whatever they did during their typical eight-hour day. Jason went into his office, which had grown way too large over the last ten years, to think about their responses.

In the early days, they had worked in a bullpen environment with people and activity all around them. There was energy, enthusiasm; it was fun. Things had changed. He had changed. As the company matured, they lost touch with their vision. They had fallen into routines that lacked energy, initiative, and creativity. In some ways, they were now the giants that others wanted to slay. From that point on, he decided to try to address the attributes that the Executive Team had given him and maybe find another metaphor to build the vision of the company around. He took the list and added another column that he titled "New Attributes."

Current attributes	New attributes (Polar opposites)
Lethargic	Energetic
Unfocused	Focused
Too big	Right size
Not motivating	Motivated
No more joy	Full of joy
Bureaucratic	Flexible
Indecisive	Decisive
Bound up	Willing to take risks
Too safe	Resilient

He thought that if the current attributes were a problem, they needed to identify the attributes that were on the complete opposite end of the spectrum.

Questions to Consider

1. If you could describe the condition of your organization in one-word attributes, what would they be?
2. Now, what are the polar opposites of these attributes?
3. Can you identify any bad habits or routines that your organization has fallen into?
4. Can you identify any bad habits or routines that you, personally, have fallen into?

PART 2

Life Is a Game of Cards

CHAPTER 2

The Power of the Unconscious Mind

The greatest impediments to changes in our traditional roles seem to lie not in the visible world of conscious intent but in the murky realm of the unconscious mind.

—Augustus Y. Napier

At this point, you must be wondering why I put so much emphasis on the use of metaphors. While it's true that metaphors can help simplify complex ideas and make them more usable in daily life, they can do so much more in helping us to change our behavior and the direction of our organizations. Like you, I have watched and listened to the media report on many successful people who have done absurd things and shipwrecked their lives. In some cases, their behavior has destroyed the lives of many people around them too, and even destroyed the organizations they faithfully served. People such as Tiger Woods, John Edwards, Rod Blagojevich, Lindsey Lohan, Jerry Sandusky, O. J. Simpson, Bernie Madoff, Dennis Kozlowski, Jim Bakker, David Sokol, Jimmy Swaggart, and Bernard J. Ebbers all engaged in undesirable behaviors that shocked everyone. I suspect that even they themselves wondered how they ended up in their particular situations. Every one of these people are gifted, talented, well-educated, with the potential to be strong, contributing members of society. Each of them, at the pinnacle of their careers, fell from grace by deviating from the norms of society and getting caught in the act. Lest ye cast the first stone, however, consider that every one of us has the potential to fall into behaviors that we would not be proud to speak of.

How did these successful people end up the way they did? I have to believe they love their families and friends, and that they had career and personal goals that were honorable. They all worked hard to get where they were. But why is it they seemed to forget the differences between right and wrong and choose a path that led each of them to destruction? What is the problem?

Limiting Behaviors

Have you ever done something without thinking, and later wished you hadn't? Almost immediately afterward, you regret your words or actions and begin a process of self-criticism and self-condemnation. You know you've hurt someone with your choice of words, but at that moment you felt almost unable to control what came out of your mouth. Have you ever failed to achieve a goal that you so desperately wanted to achieve? Sometimes it is due to a lack of motivation. Sometimes, due to a lack of focus or self-discipline, we allow distractions to divert our attention away from the things we should be doing to achieve our goals. Oftentimes when we fail, we blame it on someone else or on our circumstances rather than placing the blame where it really lies: on our own behavior.

Sometimes we find that just when we are supposed to receive a promotion or award, we say or do something that sabotages our efforts. I call these *limiting behaviors*. These are actions that seem to come from some deep dark place in our inner person that erupt in those most inopportune times. These limiting behaviors spew forth like the spray from a shaken bottle of soda when we pop the cap off. It shoots out everywhere, sticking to everything that it comes in contact with. We feel helpless to control these actions as if they have a mind of their own. In one sense they do. They have become habits that are triggered by cues or events that cause us to fall into a routine that is often debilitating. These habits are automatic, deeply imbedded in our unconscious mind, ready to leap out given the right cue or event.

Research into how the mind works has come a long way. Freudian concepts have been examined and redefined, and in some cases thrown out altogether.[1] Although experts may disagree, most contend that the unconscious mind controls somewhere between 90% and 95%[2] of our daily actions and reactions. This is a staggering thought. Just when we felt we were in control of our lives, we discover that our unconscious mind is actually at the helm. Perhaps we are not the captains of our own ships after all.

We are constantly influenced by our biases—thoughts and feelings that have taken root over time as influences have gone to seed in the fertile soil of our minds.[3] These influences come from all around us, through friends, family, news media, entertainment, print media, music, and images. As we are bombarded with input, the conscious mind is only able to handle about 40 bits of information per second, while the unconscious mind can handle up to 20,000,000 bits of information per second.[4] It's like looking at a photograph where the only part that is in focus is the very center. This is the information that the conscious mind can process. But the unconscious mind is able to see and comprehend every pixel of the photograph in complete clarity.[5] The work of the unconscious mind "allows" the conscious mind to deal with the elements in view that it focuses on. However, the unconscious mind also works to filter what the conscious mind chooses to see or comprehend.[6] Unfortunately, the unconscious mind does not always behave as we want it to. It will make choices for us that we are not aware of and can cause us to accept, focus on, and respond to things in ways that would be contrary to choices that we might make if given the time and clarity to weigh out all the facts. In addition, the unconscious mind will often "enhance" our thoughts with elements that may or may not be true.[7]

The conscious mind is where our short-term memory, and planning and analytical processes reside. This is where we weigh out pros and cons in decision-making. However, even here, bias exists. The unconscious mind is where emotions, feelings, habits, patterns of behavior, addictions, creativity, developmental stages, involuntary bodily functions, spiritual connections, and intuition reside. All of these are operating in the background of our daily mental processing.

Gaining Control

In order for us to gain some sense of control over our unconscious mind, we need to better control our inputs and change those things that influence us.[8] This process includes changing the words we hear, the images we view, the music we listen to, and the voices we allow to enter our realm of sensory input. This process requires the desire to change, the faith to believe we can change, and the discipline to follow a process that requires repetition of "good" inputs over time until our actions and reactions have rehabilitated themselves so that they truly represent our desired values. This can be accomplished through the use of metaphors, images, and sounds.[9,10]

Metaphors and sounds, such as music, create mental images that can imprint themselves on our minds by establishing cues. Repeated imprinting solidifies the image and the emotions that are associated with it. This creates an unconscious awareness that can emerge in various situations where the image is relevant to the situation at hand. The conscious mind receives the output of the unconscious mind that brings forth the image and the associated emotions and applies them to the situation by way of a routine or habitual behavior.[11] If this is the first encounter, in many cases it does not represent truth but instead represents our current reality. In a conversation between two people, this process is continually occurring.

Both parties are at the mercy of their unconscious minds and how they see the situation unfolding. Each cue causes various routines or habitual behaviors to be enacted with associated rewards. If the behavior is in response to a cue that appears confrontational, the behavior may be defensive, and the reward is the emotional satisfaction of having successfully defended itself. For example, if one party raises his voice, the other party may fall into the habitual routine of raising his voice too, and attacking the other person with personal insults. One classic example is the situation of two boys in a schoolyard who get into an argument, only to have it quickly elevate into derisive remarks about each other's mothers. The original raised voice may not have been meant to be threatening but it was received that way. Both parties may be from very different backgrounds and have very different perspectives, which can unfortunately cause significant differences of opinion leading to misunderstandings. Only through an awareness of this unconscious process can we begin to change the outcome.

Another way of dealing with poor habitual routines generated by certain cues is to *change the routine and the reward*. If someone raises her voice, and the routine is for you to immediately try to increase the volume of a response, thereby gaining the reward of having taken control of the conversation; an alternative routine might be to bring your voice down softer and lower. This still provides you with the same reward—control of the conversation—but also causes a de-escalation of the conversation, which results in a more rational discourse with better outcomes all around.

Questions to Consider

1. Can you recall a time when you said or did something that you regretted later?
2. Did you do anything to rectify the situation?
3. Do you find yourself repeating the same mistakes over and over again?
4. What bad habits or unproductive routines have you witnessed in your organization?

CHAPTER 3

Play the Hand You've Been Dealt

You've been dealt a bad hand, placed against a stacked deck!
—Words by Sage Francis, 2007, from the album, *Hell of a Year*

Our lives are a series of metaphors unfolding to paint a picture of our journey through life. I suspect if you took the time to examine your life through the lens of a metaphor, you would begin to see a pattern emerging and illustrating who you are, why you see the world as you do, and how you arrived at where you are today. Just as in the story of Jason and his record company, you could envision the attributes that reflect how you see yourself. If the metaphor that you arrive at is one that is less than complimentary such as, "My life is a toilet flushing continuously," you don't have to let it remain that way. This is what this book is about.

I discovered this principle as I processed the events in my life and began to see patterns that I was not too happy about. I could see how rejection at an early age affected my decisions and the outcomes of many potentially successful opportunities. I would often see an opportunity coming my way but because of a fear of rejection, I would sabotage it before I could experience the outcome. I would work very hard to become a final candidate for whatever it was, spelling bee champ, baseball team, or Boy Scout leader. However, because I was afraid that I would not be the one chosen, I would remove myself with a comment or an action that would disqualify me. This was my way of coping with my metaphor of, "My life is a game of cards."

As I tell my story along with the story of Jason and his record label, you will begin to see how true transformation can take place by identifying the attributes of our metaphor and changing those that are detrimental to our behavior and achievement. Sometimes it requires us to determine and act upon the polar opposite of a particular destructive attribute.

Changing the attributes of our metaphor points us toward guiding principles that, when applied, can change our destinies. Sometimes, we need to change our metaphor completely to one that is productive rather than destructive. However, to do this, we need to first examine our current and past life behaviors and experiences. It isn't easy but it can be done through the process that I lay out in the following chapters, if you are willing to allow it to take place. This might seem like a passive exercise, however, it requires active participation in the process. Through the identification and adaptation of metaphors, you can develop guiding principles that will pilot your future decisions, actions, and reactions. As you apply these guiding principles on a regular basis, you will see true and lasting transformation take place in your lives and the lives of those around you.

Developing guiding principles is usually the last step in the process. However, for the sake of clarity, I will start with guiding principles based on the metaphor, "My life is a game of cards." Later I will discuss, in depth, the process of how we arrive at our guiding principles and how we apply them on a regular basis in order for lasting change to take place. Let me begin here by playing my opening hand.

Most people will tell you that if you talk to me for more than 10 minutes, I will mention the title of a movie or the lyrics to a song. I can't help it. I was born with a song in my heart and a movie unfolding before my eyes. My accomplishments up through my early thirties were significant but not extraordinary. I had completed college, married a beautiful wife, had two beautiful children, served as a Naval Officer, earned an MBA, been a successful entrepreneur, and played small parts in television shows. Some would say that this is enough for a lifetime but for me, other than establishing a wonderful family, it had all been hollow. I lived to achieve for the sake of achievement alone. Happiness was not part of the equation. Joy was only an afterthought. It had been this way for all the years I can recall going back to my childhood growing up in Japan and later in Hawaii.

Contracting polio during the early 1950s was not uncommon. Unfortunately, it was the disease du jour for many people, both young and old. It is a debilitating disease of the central nervous system. It can literally paralyze your lungs so that you are unable to breathe on your own. Pictures of patients in iron lungs still hold strong memories for many of us. Fortunately, my polio was caught early and I experienced only partial paralysis in my legs. Naturally, this was devastating for a young boy whose life typically revolved around running, jumping, and playing. For me, the boundaries of the crib that I lived in defined my life into early childhood. The walls were bars that kept me in. They were my looking glass to the possible but the improbable. I lived in a hospital that included others who had been dealt a similar hand.

I had a small friction bus toy that I played with every day. It took me to places far away where I experienced an imaginary life beyond my crib. This life included total mobility. I could run, jump, and play. I knew the wind and the rain as my companions while I raced about life in my magic bus with a total abandonment, only to be brought back to the reality of my crummy hand by a nurse coming to change my diapers.

For some reason, unbeknownst to me, I was taken to a foster family on weekends. I remember they had two children, a boy of about 5 and a girl of about 7 years of age. Although a couple of years older, the boy was my best and only friend. Since I was unable to walk due to the paralysis, I'm sure our playtimes were a bit subdued. I remember distinctly him telling me that I was lucky to be going to live with rich Americans. At the time I didn't know what he was talking about but apparently an adoption was on my horizon. My hand appeared to be improving.

Physical therapy had helped strengthen my legs, and I was able to walk but with a pronounced limp. At night my legs would twist into severe cramps, causing me to cry out as the muscles rebelled against the work that they had to do during my waking hours. Each day my legs grew stronger and I could easily stand and move about a room, eventually becoming able to run, albeit not very fast. The first time I saw the movie *Forest Gump*, with Tom Hanks (remember what I said about the first 10 minutes with me?), the scene with him running down the road as his leg braces started to come apart really hit me. The new freedom that he was experiencing as he ran from the bullies was something that I could relate to.

There Is Always Another Card to Draw

The trip to the airport when I was four years old was quiet. It was a small regional airport on the Southern island of Kyushu, Japan. My nurse, who

I called "Oneeson," meaning elder sister, sat holding me in the taxi. Upon arrival, she carried me to the steps of the airplane and handed me up to the Japanese pilot of the twin-prop cargo plane. Oneeson and I cried as I was ripped from my world of bars and busses, and an occasional diaper changing. I knew something significant was happening but I was unable to relate it to my young friend's comment that he had made several weeks earlier. All I knew was that a man that I didn't recognize, in a cap and uniform was carrying me into a large contraption that made a lot of noise. He placed me in a jump seat with boxes, cargo netting, and other supplies all around me. I'm not sure why it was a cargo plane, but I'm sure I felt like a piece of cargo.

At the time, I was wearing everything that I owned. I looked like an overstuffed teddy bear. I still have the plastic sandals that I was wearing on that flight. They are a reminder of a time when everything was outside of my control, a time when cards were being played that positioned me for either success or failure in life. The hand that I had been dealt was a losing hand but if I could just draw another card, it could turn that hand into a winning one.

If I strained my neck, there was a small porthole where I was able to see out. After the plane was airborne, white wisps of clouds engulfed the porthole and then thinned out as we rose above the clouds into clear sky. Although I was totally engrossed with the beautiful scenery with its blue, white, and occasional patches of green rice paddies below, the trip seemed to take forever. The landing in Yokosuka was uneventful, and I knew this part of the adventure was over. However, I was headed for many more surprises. The pilot released me from my buckles and carried me to a waiting couple at the bottom of the stairs. Remember, this was before motorized, elevated walkways. In those days, the ground crew would push a metal staircase on wheels to the side of the plane and passengers would climb down to the tarmac and proceed to the terminal.

The woman looked like my foster mother, beautiful and easily Japanese. The man, however, was strange looking. He did not look like any Japanese man that I had ever seen. He had an incredible white smile and eyes the color of the sky. He lifted me up on his shoulders as we walked away from the plane. I was in a state of shock and crying. I could tell the couple was trying to talk to me but in a language that I had never heard.

As they carried me to the parking lot, we approached a powder blue and white 1955 Chevy Bellaire convertible. Of course, I didn't know what kind of car it was at the time, but I stopped crying the moment that I knew it belonged to them. I'm sure I was thinking about my young friend's words about going to live with rich Americans.

Unfortunately, the part about their being rich turned out to be less than accurate. However, I would never trade them for the wealthiest parents in the entire world. Although they were not financially rich, they were rich in love and gave me that, as well as unconditional acceptance and a life that I could never have imagined. The deck had been reshuffled, and my hand was beginning to improve.

Learn the Rules of the Game

I graduated from high school a year early thanks to a California educational initiative in the early 1960s that established progressive schools where students could take exams and skip grades. I could have skipped two grades but my parents were rightfully concerned about my socialization into a much older peer group. I worked hard in school. I was the kid that always sat in front and raised my hand every time the teacher asked questions. I finished my work usually before anyone else, and still earned top grades. However, I know the teachers were irritated with me because I also tried to keep everyone laughing. In the sixth grade, I was voted most entertaining by the faculty. I thought it was a good thing but I suspect it was the only thing my teachers could give me that acknowledged any positive attributes I brought to the classroom educational experience. Needless to say, I enjoyed the attention.

As the son of a career military man, we moved a lot. I must have attended over a dozen schools by the time I graduated from high school. During my last year of high school, I found myself connecting with the wrong crowd. I started drinking and partying pretty heavily. There was a growing emptiness that I was trying to fill with alcohol and good times.

While the military draft and a war in Southeast Asia was taking many of my friends, I went off to college at Ohio State University, mainly because I didn't know what else to do. Every night dinner conversations were hushed as the news anchors gave the body counts for the day.

The Vietnam War, or police action as some politicians were still calling it, was first and foremost the topic of the day. Being young, I gravitated toward antiwar groups and the rhetoric that accompanied them. My antiwar activities, however, involved merely hanging out at antiwar rallies, mainly for the partying that accompanied any unified gathering of young people. It was like a rock concert on steroids.

I drifted from party to party, skipping classes whenever I thought I could get away with it. I was living for each day without concern for my future or the consequences of my actions. The more the emptiness grew, the more I sought to drown it in beer and parties. Finally, I received a notice from the Registrar's office stating that I was being placed on academic probation. I left Ohio State after one year. I had played a wild card and lost.

That summer I moved back home with my parents, got a job at Sears, and tried to figure out what to do with my life. Eventually, I went the way of my father and joined the Navy. This decision came because I felt my options had come down to this and only this. In some ways, I felt like Richard Gere in *Officer and a Gentleman*. In the movie, he had grown up pretty independently. After going to college and trying to do several kinds of jobs, he had pretty much decided that the Navy was the only thing left for him. His father had been a career sailor as well. For him, it was his last chance to make something of himself. Like him, I felt I had nowhere left to go.

I hadn't seriously considered the rules of life. I frittered away my options for the future in exchange for the short-term joy and satisfaction of the immediate. I never thought to find a mentor. In fact, the use of mentors, at that time, was not a widely publicized way of learning the rules. Most of my generation was distrustful of older people. We were stupid and prideful. We should have recognized that the rules of life were many and complex, and to listen to others who had gone before us would have been the best thing we could have done at the time. Many heartaches and lost hands could have been avoided.

Questions to Consider

1. Can you think of a limiting behavior that seems to stunt your emotional growth or prevent your professional advancement?

2. Based upon this limiting behavior, is there a metaphor that comes to mind that illustrates this behavior? For example, if your limiting behavior is constantly starting to speak before the other person completes their sentence or thought, your metaphor might be, "I'm a stomping elephant." This signifies that you stomp on the things others say with little care or appreciation for what they are saying.

3. Can you identify the attribute of this limiting behavior? For example, if your limiting behavior is the one stated in the previous question, the attribute might be a lack of careful listening skills, or a lack of respect or appreciation for other's opinions.

CHAPTER 4

See Your Winning Hand

Where there is no vision, my people perish . . .
—Proverbs 29:18

In the game of life there are winners and losers. Sometimes the only thing separating the two is that winners see themselves as winners. I remember upon graduating from high school, being asked at the tender age of 17, "Now, what will you do with the rest of your life?" I felt like Dustin Hoffman in *The Graduate*. Although there was no Mrs. Robinson, I still felt the pressure of being required to answer the question. Because I worked in gas stations most of my years of high school I replied, "I just want to pump gas the rest of my life." It was not the answer the person who was asking the question wanted to hear nor was it the answer that I really wanted to give. I was at a loss with the question. I hadn't seriously considered it. I loved working on cars but couldn't see myself doing that for a living. In fact, it was a challenge for me to see myself doing any one thing for the rest of my life. Little was I to know that this was the very trait that would establish and fuel a vision for my life.

Vision is a funny thing. Some say it is our preferred future. Some see it as that thing we want to become. Others see it as the lens to view our future. In my early years after high school, I don't remember having thought of the word or the concept and if I did, I would not have entertained the idea for more than a moment. Vision, for me, was what people had when they were on bad drugs. It was temporary, fleeting, unattainable, and usually led to weeks or months in an insane asylum. This was not my preferred future.

In a game of cards, all the players try to visualize what the other players have in their hands. If they are good, they have counted the cards that have already been played, weighed the probabilities that key cards are being held by various players, and assessed how their own cards will stack up against a hand that might play out as they thought it would. Naturally, unless one is a pro with total recall, most of the time probability does not play out. The cards being played come as a surprise, and you end up losing or tossing your cards in. It is disappointing. You may have rendered the perfect poker face while never giving any sense of your actual hand, but chance can be a cruel taskmaster.

If you live your life as one chance after another, you will live it without purpose, always being the dog wagged by its own tail. Any goals that you may stumble upon never materialize because your attention span toward accomplishing these goals lacks wisdom, strategy, and energy. You are at the mercy of every idea or whim that floats by. You will be tugged back and forth without direction. You will have no target to aim at, nothing guiding your trajectory.

The Navy, for me, was the dog, and I was the tail. I did what the dog told me to do. I was an obedient tail. Now, I'm not saying that the Navy didn't help me; it did. However, I still didn't have a vision for my life and spent four years doing my job, enjoying the immediacy of life, and not preparing for anything in particular. Even when I left the Navy, I was wandering aimlessly. I had the GI Bill that would pay some of my college expenses, but I knew I would have to work to supplement my income. I was happy to leave the Navy, but still felt that my future was something that I had no vision for. I lacked passion and didn't know what to do so I went back to college.

This time around, I was motivated to complete my college degree. Having worked mindlessly the previous four years, I enjoyed putting my mind back to work. However, because I really didn't have a passion, I studied things that I was interested in but not passionate about. I really had no passion for anything in particular and therefore I had no vision. My interests were broad and varied, but I lacked purpose. I didn't see how the hand that I'd been dealt would help me in any way.

When You Lack Vision Follow Your Instincts

Because of a lack of passion for anything in particular, I returned to what I knew, how to be entertaining. I channeled my energies into singing and acting. I was pursing one of those college degrees that essentially would not open any doors. For some reason, it never dawned on me that I would need talent. Well, I was an adequate actor and landed some bit television parts here and there. They were nothing to write about and paid very little. I enjoyed being on stage or in front of the camera, but the enjoyment was only for the moment as it fed my ego. I really didn't want to be a career actor, but I couldn't see myself doing anything else at the time. I didn't have a clear vision for acting and just enjoyed the camaraderie of my fellow actors during rehearsals and performances.

Upon graduating from college, I struggled to find a job. I knew I needed a career but had no vision for what that should be. I was again at that place where I couldn't see options. I went back to the Navy recruiter. I applied and got accepted to Officer Candidate School and left for Newport, Rhode Island. My fellow officer candidates for the most part were motivated. Most of them saw themselves one day commanding their own ships. They were passionate about this. I didn't understand it. For me, this was just a job, not an adventure. I did well but lacked the passion they had.

Studying calculus, engineering, and navigation were interesting but just part of the job of a naval officer. What I really enjoyed was studying leadership and understanding the dynamics of people working together. Although this was mostly in the context of shipboard life, I could see so many connections to how organizations functioned. I began to understand more clearly why people acted the way they did. I saw the reasons for various behaviors and developed an understanding of how to bring the best out in people. I was beginning to find something I could be passionate about and developing a vision for my life. I saw the potential for a winning hand.

After I received my commission as an ensign and was sent to my first ship, I was able to put into practice all that I had learned. I was adequate in most things but did really well in ship handling. I loved being on the bridge of the ship underway, making decisions, giving engine and rudder commands, and working with the men and women on watch with me. I loved the teamwork that went into running the ship well. The precision, the collegiality, and the discipline all fed my growing vision to understand leadership and management better. I was becoming passionate about this, and had become an intense student of the fields of leadership, management, and organizational behavior. I would find myself dissecting various situations, trying to understand the motives behind each player. I tried to see what cards they were holding that gave them some sense of superiority or strategic advantage. I watched as scenarios played out daily and later reflected on the ways the various hands were played.

My background in acting had prepared me well for this. As an actor, one must understand his or her motivations as well as the motivations of others in the scene and then respond to them. When this is done well, the scene becomes real. The actors are no longer acting; they have become their characters. Their characters have come alive with their own purposes. They have captured the vision of the characters and put that vision into practice. They are motivated by the vision, and all actions are initiated in pursuit of that vision. This is when acting tries to imitate life, and to some degree it does. However, it short-circuits the pursuit of vision by distilling actions down to the most essential ones that are consistent with the vision and the motivations that accompany it. Anything else is superfluous to the scene and would make the act way too long for any audience. The audience gets to see the vision for each character unfold in less than two or three hours. Each character has a preferred future that is revealed in its most honest, albeit abbreviated sense.

Life is not so pure in this way. Other activities that muddy vision or are not related to the vision are acted upon daily. There is no timeframe to get everyone out of the theater, or to the intermission or commercial break. Life can drag on with all its complications and diversions. Vision can get lost.

Focus Can Clarify Your Vision

Have you ever seen those visual puzzles that ask, "What do you see in this picture?" I always chuckle at what we must look like going through the facial gymnastics while trying to identify the hidden shape. Our heads turn, our eyes squint, and our pupils dilate as they trying to capture the hidden image in the picture. It might be Jesus or the facial profile of an old woman. But the exercise may not be futile.

Sailors at sea spend a great deal of time looking at the horizon, trying to see the beginning shape of things. In fact, we are taught the shape of various ships by looking at silhouettes on flash cards. We do this so that if and when we spot these ships, we are careful to avoid colliding with them. Accidents at sea can happen very quickly, and can be difficult to avoid unless actions are taken early enough on to steer clear of oncoming ships and other obstacles.

Navy ships are the only moving platform that I know of that keeps lookouts on watch 24/7. There is always one lookout at the front of the ship and one at the back. These are called the bow and stern respectively. In addition, there are usually one or more stationed higher up on both sides, as well as on the bridge. In fact, the entire bridge team usually has binoculars and spends considerable amount of time peering into the distance.

Being a lookout is one of the most important jobs aboard ships. It is usually not considered a full-time job but is part of a collateral duty that junior enlisted sailors must assume as part of their underway watch station. The young sailors who have performed best by spotting things early are usually assigned to critical teams underway. Various evolutions, such as sailing into port, require the very best sailors in all critical positions. On naval ships this particular evolution is called "sea and anchor detail." The team chosen for this detail is usually sent to their stations long before the ship enters port. The lookouts' responsibility, beyond spotting ships, boats, and other obstacles, is to spot familiar land formations, buoys, and other navigational aids so that the ship can be sailed into port safely and efficiently. These lookouts have demonstrated a high degree of ability to focus, to block out all distractions, and to concentrate on what they are seeing. This ability has saved many a ship and the sailors onboard.

Focusing on your vision requires this same intense ability to concentrate. You must learn to see Jesus in the picture and block out the old woman. Every manner of distraction will be thrown at you as you try to focus. Your ability and willingness to concentrate will be challenged. How many times have we all found ourselves listening to someone talk about a very important issue and recognized that our minds were wandering as we thought about getting gas on the way home, or picking up coffee creamer at the grocery store so that we could enjoy our morning coffee the way we liked it prepared? We must remain attentive, giving important things in life our complete focus and commitment.

Stop Trying to Multitask

So many well-meaning people have told us that multitasking is a great skill. When we are able to do this, we can be more efficient, more productive, and more promotable. Generations X, Y, Z, and AO (always on), are touted as masters of multitasking. We older adults have watched as they did their homework, watched television on their computers, and texted on their smart phones, all at the same time. We assumed that they were doing these tasks with some degree of proficiency. Unfortunately, recent research has shown that this is incorrect. One task, like texting with friends, will take preference over another task. These other tasks are often relegated to level where these young people do just enough to get a passing grade or gain some general sense of what happened in the episode. The deep thinking, the intense focusing is nonexistent.

When we are multitasking, we are not really giving any of our tasks our complete focus. The bombardment to our senses in a multitasking environment does not allow us to see with clarity our goals or the best way to achieve them. We find ourselves settling on the process of achievement that engages the least amount of energy, information, and perspective. Unfortunately, because of this, the results are always less than stellar. We simply accept the consequences and learn to be satisfied with this. What suffers is our vision. Without focus, our vision can mutate into something that we never intended it to be. Ultimately, we never achieve the vision that we longed for and never fulfill our purpose in life.

It takes deliberate practice to tune out the distractions and tune into accomplishing the vision. The way to begin this is to embrace purpose in your life. Discover why you exist. What is your role in this world? What values will you live by? What boundaries will define your actions? Who will you allow and acknowledge joining you on this journey? For me, this last question helped me to define the others.

Questions to Consider

1. Recall a time when you acted on your instincts and were right in doing so.
2. What things during the day cause you to lose focus?
3. Do you try to multitask? If so, what things do you try to do simultaneously?

CHAPTER 5

Playing Cards Doesn't Have to Be a Solo Sport

Though one may be overpowered, two can defend themselves. A cord of three strands is not quickly broken.

—Ecclesiastes 4:12, NIV

Having grown up as a military brat, and for the most part, without siblings (my sister was adopted when I was 12, and we lived in the same household for only five years), I learned to entertain myself. I would spend countless hours in my room building models, creating alternate realities, or playing famous war heroes. My room was my shop, my space capsule, and my battlefield. I was perfectly happy being by myself, tackling life's problems, and discovering new things through books and television. I did spend time outdoors, but it was usually spent trying to develop friendships.

Moving every three to four years as my father was posted to another command required me to hold on to relationships loosely. I had to find a safe place in my heart to allow others in but only to the degree that when the inevitable happened, a move to another place, I would not be devastated by the interruption. Naturally, the depths of my relationships were probably suspect. I could play the part of a close friend but only in so far as feigning a genuine interest in their affairs.

When we arrived at a new home, I would spend a great deal of time developing friendships. I knew these had a beginning and an end but I was determined to make the best of it. I had developed behaviors that allowed me to be engaging but still allowed me to maintain some distance. I learned to protect my heart and emotions by not seeming to take anything seriously. I liked to make others laugh and have fun, but this prevented me from becoming close. I played on sports teams but was never very good at it. I didn't like having to rely on others.

Sometimes we think we can do everything on our own. We believe in our own strength and our own tenacity to overcome all obstacles. We trust our instincts and barricade them from others to preserve our environment. However, life should not be played this way. In many games of cards, players play their hand without the benefit of someone helping them. This can be satisfying when one wins but frustrating when one loses. What I didn't realize when I was young was that some card games allow people to play together in teams.

Strengthen Your Hand Through Teamwork

While attending Ohio State University, I was introduced to a card game called Euchre. This game is played with only the tens through the kings and the aces. Everyone played it, sometimes at the expense of studying. You could see Euchre games being played in every dorm room, every lobby, every cafeteria, and even in the classrooms and libraries on campus. Euchre is played in teams of two. In some Euchre circles, signals are expected and allowed. These signals are highly developed and refined with a partner who is expected to be loyal to the partnership. Members of good teams seem to have a sixth sense that guides their plays. The cards are played in a predictable sequence with one partner helping the other so that, in the end, the team wins the game. They are both committed to the outcome or the vision of winning, and they both know they are contributing something of value to the vision. They are united in their journey.

I was perfectly satisfied playing solo sports, particularly surfing, and SCUBA diving. SCUBA diving, although usually done with a buddy, is still a solo sport. Your buddy is there, not as a team member but as a person you hope you can rely on in the event of an emergency such as running out of air.

As I advanced up the training ladder to the level of PADI Open Water SCUBA Instructor, I learned many underwater tasks and how to teach them to others. Teaching is a solo sport to some degree, but I discovered in time that I could be more effective working with a team.

The first basic SCUBA course that I taught after being certified as an instructor had about 30 aspiring Jacque Cousteau types. In the classroom they hung on to every word I said, taking extensive notes, and asking numerous questions. Sometimes, I would enjoy scaring them by telling a personal shark encounter story. This elevated my ego as they saw me as the invincible shark warrior. However, in the open water, I could no longer rely on my invincibility to control, and more importantly, to protect my students from making deadly mistakes.

During the final dive of the Basic Open-Water SCUBA Certification course, I required a 100-foot bounce dive, meaning we would swim down to 100 feet, take a look around, and ascend to the surface. I did this so that the students' curiosity would be satisfied when they saw that the grey, cold environment at that depth was nothing to write home about. In the more advanced courses, I would have my students simulate running out of air at that depth, by taking their regulators out of their mouths and swimming to the surface on just the air they had in their lungs. This is called a free ascent. For new divers, this is too dangerous. Nevertheless, I would take my class down to a 100-foot ledge and line them up along the ledge so that they could peer into the grey imposing depth beyond.

With 30 students, it was not safe for me to take them on this dive alone. I had many friends who were advanced divers, and they volunteered to work as part of my team to ensure the safety of my students. I assigned one advanced diver to hover over and just behind 3–5 students as they stood on the ledge. Everything seemed safe and under control so this was merely a safety precaution. Everyone looked calm and composed, this being their fourth ocean dive.

I had them conduct exercises, such as taking their regulators out of their mouths and returning them, and taking their masks off and putting them back on while clearing the water out. They had done this dozens of times in the pool and on previous shallow water dives. While they were doing this, I noticed that one of my students, a young lady, seemed to be overly enjoying this last exercise. In that moment, without her mask on, she leaned forward and started swimming frantically for the bottom, which leveled off at 200 feet. I spun around, kicking my fins as hard and fast as I could, I chased her. I was able to grab her falling mask on the way down and was reaching out as far as my arms could extend to grab her flailing fins from behind.

When I reached her, we had hit about 130 feet, the approximate safe limit for compressed air SCUBA equipment. I grabbed her, turned her around, and headed back to the rest of the class. I could see a calm, joyous expression on her face. I knew that she had succumbed to nitrogen narcosis; a potentially debilitating but not necessarily fatal condition if someone is there to assist. Susceptibility to nitrogen narcosis can occur for many people approaching the 80–100-foot depth. It is like drinking a shot or two of your favorite liquor. It makes you feel invincible, like you can dive to the deepest depth or do the most outrageous things safely. On one occasion, this happened to me but as soon as I felt the giddiness, I moved into shallow water, which alleviated the problem. We swam swiftly but safely back toward the rest of the class standing on the 100-foot ledge.

On the way back, I had a moment of suppressed panic. Was the class okay? Had something disastrous occurred while I was chasing after the young lady? As the class came into focus I could see the tips of the bottom portions of their fins as they protruded slightly over the edge of the ledge. I started counting pairs, 1, 2, 3, and up to 29. Whew! As the young lady and I reached the 100-foot ledge, I noticed behind each small group of three to five students, my loyal and committed team members cautiously watching, ready to respond at a moment's notice to any emergency that might befall their designated students. I learned the importance of teamwork that day.

Working as a SCUBA instructor at a local dive shop, I spent my time underwater six of seven days per week. On the seventh day after church, I rested by paddling out on my surfboard and catching waves. I loved sitting on the water, straddling my board, and looking at the horizon while trying to spot the building of a swell. When I spotted a wave approaching, I along with everyone in my immediate vicinity would feverously paddle to what we thought would be the perfect spot to catch the wave. When I caught the wave, inevitably, there was someone next to me trying to ride it as well. Good manners and protocol dictate that the surfer closest to the breaking white water has the right of way and others should give preference to that person. This is not necessarily teamwork but sometimes it can feel like it especially when the sun is shining, the water is warm and clear, and everyone is in a good mood. We worked together, honoring the values and protocols of surfing so that we each had a day that we would remember fondly.

On one occasion, while surfing with a couple of veteran surfer friends and one friend who was experiencing his first time on a surfboard, we saw a large shark cross in front of us. We were all paddling abreast of each other to catch a wave, when the shark's fin broke the surface about five feet in front of my board. I immediately reacted by pulling my hands out of the water and lifting my feet and calves up perpendicular to my body, putting my whole balance on my solar plexus. As I watched the shark pass, I saw next to me, out of the corner of my right eye, my novice surfer friend starting to panic. His board was shaking and he was about to fall off. Almost in perfect synchronization, two of us on both sides of my panicking friend reached out to stabilize his surfboard. We talked to him calmly to help him regain his composure as we gingerly reached back into the water to paddle in.

We worked instinctively in that moment of crisis. We understood each other's personalities and skills. We bounced encouraging words back and forth, utilizing metaphors such as, "This is a piece of cake," and "You handled that like Superman!" We were able to turn the potential disaster into a few moments of chuckles knowing that my panicking friend had experienced something that he could tell his grandkids one day. He survived a shark encounter. Although, in this instance, our team was very small, I discovered that the sharing of responsibility could be a very rewarding experience.

Our teamwork was greatly appreciated but, as far as I know, it was the last time my friend ever went surfing. Sometimes you can win the hand but lose friends in the process.

Key Team Members Can Help You Achieve Your Vision

As a musician, I played in many garage bands growing up. Needless to say, they were mostly disappointing and frustrating experiences. Musicians are not known for punctuality or a willingness to function as a team. We try but because most musical instrument practice occurs in solo settings, musicians can have a hard time performing in an ensemble. After many attempts to form and perform in a band, I set out on a not so successful solo career. I played a few gigs but couldn't see myself doing this forever. I tried to maintain my band during this time, setting up regular practices, doing the marketing, and writing songs. I found that I did most of the business of the group and I was pretty good at it. A keyboardist friend of mine commented one day that I should consider managing artists. I asked him why he thought that? He said that I was the only musician that he knew who was organized. I suspect this was due to my years as a naval officer. I was not particularly intrigued by this idea until I started receiving phone calls from a number of musician friends who had heard that I was taking on clients.

Before I knew it, I had several clients who were quite notable in my area, and I was booking showrooms and lounges. This was a solo venture, and I was enjoying making a good living in music. However, because I was alone, my productivity was limited. There were just so many artists I could represent and do it well. Anymore than that, and I would have to shortchange them and not give proper attention to their careers.

One day while I was feeding pigeons at the park, a good friend who recently had a hit record came up to me and said he and his music partner needed some help. He had a manager, named Dillon, and they were hoping that I would talk with him to see if we might work together to help their careers. Dillon and I met and discussed the idea of merging as equal partners. It seemed like the right thing to do, and before long, we controlled most of the showrooms and lounges in the city. We had a strong stable of artists. We started a record label, a television show, and a production company, and we were finding ourselves quite successful. In addition, we were gaining a solid reputation for taking care of our artists when other managers were not as generous and caring.

I found that our teamwork allowed us to multiply our efforts. We were focused on a common vision and had value systems that were identical. We were second-guessing each other's responses and had become genuinely good friends. We had also become the perfect Euchre team. Not all teammates will be onboard with the vision. Some will try to take advantage of others and the situation. Good teammates may be difficult to find but when you do, make sure you bring them aboard.

Recognize Good Teammates When They Cross Your Path

Another natural outlet for my desire to entertain was radio. There was work available, and I was fortunate to have discovered this early in my career. I built up a solid resume of radio jobs from sales, to on-air per-sonality, to program manager. I was enjoying my airtime and the ability to share my thoughts with a larger audience. I spent most of my day in and around the station even after my on air shift was over. There was a small bookstore down the hall from the radio station, and when I could steal a few minutes away, I would wander down there and browse the bookshelves.

Having had a disastrous first marriage when I was much younger, I was reluctant to allow anyone else to join Team Jim. One day, while scanning the new books that had come in, I noticed a beautiful young lady at the counter. I hadn't seen her before. Walking up to the counter I asked her a question, and her reply came across short and not so sweet. I wondered if she was just having a bad day? Her response, however, only spurred me on in subsequent encounters to try to develop a friendly conversation.

One day, while trying to think of something to say, my friend the owner of the bookstore, said, "Why don't you just ask her out?" His voice was sufficiently loud enough to catch the ear of this young lady. With a perplexed and slightly embarrassed expression, I did so. She accepted, and we went on our first date that evening.

Laurie became my best friend. We spent most of our waking hours together or in close proximity. She would sit outside the broadcast booth waiting for my shift to end. We would go to the beach every weekend. While she sat on the beach reading, I was out in the line up surfing. I'd come in for lunch and paddle out again until it was time to take her home. She was and has always been there for me. She brought out the best in me and continues to do so, and I hope that I've done so for her as well. This is what good teammates do. We were married the next summer. My hand was definitely improving.

Bad Habits Are Hard to Break

Bad habits become glaringly obvious in the early days of marriage. For men, these are particularly difficult to identify and even more difficult to admit to and break free from. One of my buddies in college had a habit of breathing in a quick snort of air when he was ready to bluff in a game of

Texas Hold-em. Everything would be deftly quiet, as the cards were dealt around the table. Calvin, not his real name, would lift his cards carefully, gently spreading them open so that only he could see the concealed panorama, and ever so slightly snort if he had a bad hand that he was going to bet on. I would listen for this routine with each hand. I'm not sure others knew this bad habit that Calvin had developed, but it allowed me to work his bluff in my favor. He could not resist trying to draw someone into his trap because the emotional and psychological reward when he was successful was obvious on his face. The reward was almost like a drug that beckoned Calvin to carry out the bluff even when all odds were against him. I saw him lose one hand after another trying to work his bluff each time. I thought he even looked forward to bad cards just so that he could engage his bluff, all the while hoping to experience the emotional and psychological high of trapping his opponents and moving them to fold their hands. Naturally, after everyone folded, he never showed his bluff hands with the exception of one time, when he inadvertently laid his cards face up as he gathered the chips to himself. From that point on, I watched and listened for his bluff cue, and when I heard it, I stayed in the game knowing that I had at least one opponent that I did not have to be concerned with.

Having gotten married to Laurie when I was 32, I had developed some bad habits. One that most men have is leaving the toilet seat up. When a man enters a bathroom, water closet, or toilet, whatever your culture calls it, he typically walks over to a stand up device. These devices do not require you to touch anything apart from your own body. There is something that is particularly distasteful about having to touch the urinal or toilet lid particularly in a public facility. Guys just want to go in, take care of business, and exit with little or no contact with our environment. We don't mind washing our hands, which requires touching the faucet, but that is very different than lifting a toilet seat or lid.

At home, we like to keep things uncomplicated. We figure leaving the lid and seat up allows us the liberty to remain uncontaminated from the germs of our environment. We can quickly move to the device, do our business, step back, and move away. In that moment, we experience the cathartic joy of unencumbered release. Well, for some reason women like to have the seat down, probably for all the same reasons that men prefer the seat up. When we got married, I had to develop better habits; putting the seat back down was one of them.

As I mentioned earlier, habits run in loops. There is first a cue, something that motivates us to engage in a routine. The routine comes next, followed by a reward. The reward in the card game example was the joy that Calvin experienced having bluffed his opponents. In the previous example of the toilet seat, the reward was the cathartic joy of unencumbered release.

Habits are difficult to change. The best way to change them is to either change the reward or the routine as cues are very difficult to change since they are usually beyond your control. In the toilet seat example, over time, I added to my routine the element of lifting the seat and lowering it back down upon completion. My reward was lessened somewhat, in that now my routine was encumbered with the activity of engaging the pivot points of the toilet mechanism but the positive reward or reinforcement of my physical satisfaction remained. In addition, I gained a negative reinforcement by not having to anger my beautiful bride. Individuals as well as organizations have routines or habits that are detrimental to their daily functioning and ultimately to their growth and success.

Questions to Consider

1. When you have been on teams in the past, what did you find successful about working in a team environment? What did you find less than successful?
2. What elements would you consider makes for a productive team?
3. Think about your worst habit. What routine does it involve, what reward do you receive, and what cues or prompts you to follow this routine?
4. What routines are carried out in your organization? Are they positive or negative routines? Why?

PART 3

The Art of Metaformation

CHAPTER 6

Metaframing: Structuring Metaphors

Bye, bye, Miss American Pie
Drove my Chevy to the levee
But the levee was dry
Them good ol'boys were drinkin' whiskey and rye
Singing "this'll be the day that I die
This'll be the day that I die."

—"Miss American Pie," Words and Music by
Don McClean, 1971

I'm not sure whether, before reading this book, you've ever thought much about metaphors. The entire 1970s song "Miss American Pie," was a series of metaphors that brought forth a message of simpler times gone by. We use metaphors all the time when we say things such as, "This rain is worse than a hail of bullets," or "Life is going to be clear sailing from now on." The first compares a driving rainstorm using the imagery of bullets flying and the impact they can have. The second compares an upcoming season of life that is seemingly carefree with the imagery of sailing on a beautiful clear day. Each delivers a distinct sensory input that brings real meaning to the things being compared.

In the first example, a "hail of bullets" is the greater or stronger domain while the rain is the lesser domain. Domain refers to the two things being compared. The stronger domain is called the "vehicle," and the lesser domain is called the "target." The vehicle drives the attributes that it represents to the target thereby, strengthening the target. Some refer to the vehicle as the "base," however; I prefer the sense of movement that the term "vehicle" represents. In the second example, "clear sailing" is the vehicle or stronger domain while "life" is the target or lesser domain. This concept of vehicle and target is essentially true in most metaphors and will be treated that way throughout this book.

Asymmetry of Metaphors

This imbalance expresses an asymmetry or imbalance between the vehicle and target. The vehicle is stronger than the target. Relationally, the vehicle contributes something of value to the target but not the other way around. This value may be in simply adding clarity to the target image. The target is where one begins and the recipient of the added value. It is only with the added value brought to it from the vehicle that the target benefits. This asymmetry begins with a driving up from the target to the vehicle as the vehicle reaches back and contributes an attribute of value to the target, as shown in figure below (Figure 6.1).

This driving up from target to vehicle and the returning added value by way of the attribute is what makes metaphors so powerful. Consider the following metaphor, "The young boy's strength was that of a thousand pulling horses as he lifted the car off of his mother." As you read this, it becomes apparent that the young boy was engaging in a feat that was beyond the capabilities of a normal boy. The thousand pulling horses, which is the vehicle, magnify this feat by attributing superhuman power to the young boy. The power of the vehicle to infer back to the target, the idea of a young boy lifting the car off of his mother, has immediate and

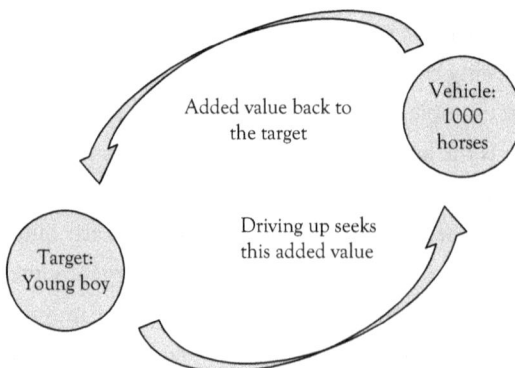

Figure 6.1. The Action Metaphor.

direct impact on the meaning of the metaphor changing the visual image forever. This is what I call "picturesquing." This is different than visualizing in that it recognizes emotional activity and includes emotions in the overall sensory response.

Action-Oriented Metaphors

Metaphors can create action in the way that orders given by an admiral cause all within hearing distance to scramble. Metaphors can bring clarity and belief in the future that can drive the current reality into a new arena of possibilities. Which would be a more powerful image, "We need to increase sales by 15% in the next quarter," versus "Our sales should look like we are we are on fire and unloading everything we've got, and this should be reflected in a sales increase of 15% or more in the coming quarter." Both statements include a quantitative value, but the second statement paints a more powerful image through the addition of the metaphor comparing sales that are burning with the speed and ferocity of a fire.

The second half of this metaphor signifies a benchmark that is now more possible because of the preceding half. When something is on fire, the features that are represented include: (1) urgency, (2) feverish activity, and (3) making every effort to "put the fire out." This creates an emotional force that is not included in the first statement, "We need to increase sales by 15% in the next quarter." If anything, this statement evokes fear and apprehension rather than action.

The Importance of Structural Alignment

The act of metaframing, or discovering and developing a metaphor that is appropriate for the situation, requires us to consider several things; (1) the relational structure, (2) the object, (3) the desired attributes. This involves finding "structural alignment" of two or more structured representations containing objects, their relations, and their attributes, along with the relationship between their relations so that the common elements in the representations are mapped onto each other. This is part of the process called structural mapping,[1] which includes finding commonalities and projecting inferences. This might sound complex but it is relatively simple to do. I'll present it here briefly but discuss this more in-depth in a later chapter.

An easy example to recognize structural alignment is in comparing the atom, which includes a nucleus surrounded by electrons, and the solar system, which includes the sun surrounded by planets. The relational structure is the same as the sun relates to the nucleus, both in the center, the planets relate to the atoms that revolve around the sun and the nucleus respectively. This is important so that when you consider metaphors, you are using vehicles that properly match the target. This prevents confusion when thinking about or articulating the metaphor. For the leader, this is critical since you want every message to be clear and without any chance of misinterpretation.

Comparing objects without considering their relationship can create a metaphor that is not structurally aligned. "That gossipy woman is a star falling from the sky." The objects of the woman and the star have nothing in common in this context. However, consider, "That gossipy woman is a humming bird flitting about from flower to flower." A relationship exists between the woman and the humming bird through the implied attribute of the gossipy nature pictured in the woman moving about from person to person as the humming bird moves about from flower to flower. It is the implied attribute that helps define the relationship of the objects. If the original sentence were, "The young actress is a star falling from the sky," then the relational structure would be aligned because the implied attribute is that of a young actress who is peaking in her career early and is on the downward spiral of her notoriety as a star that is falling from the sky and is soon to be extinguished. Metaphors have many hidden nuggets that can reveal themselves through careful investigation.

Learning Reinforcement Exercise

1. In this metaphor, circle the word or phrase that identifies the target.
   a. This rain is worse than a hail of bullets.
2. In this metaphor, circle the word(s) that identify the vehicle
   a. Life is going to be clear sailing from now on.
3. Which has greater power? (Circle)   Target   Vehicle
4. Which gains the greater benefit? (Circle) Target   Vehicle

5. In this metaphor, circle the word that implies the attribute of the horses.

   a. The young boy's strength was like that of a thousand pulling horses as he lifted the car off of his mother.

6. Which metaphor has structural alignment? (Circle)

   a. That gossipy woman is a star falling from the sky.

   b. That gossipy woman is a humming bird flitting about from flower to flower.

Answers are in italics:

1. In this metaphor, circle the word(or phrase) that identifies the target.

   a. This *rain* is worse than a hail of bullets.

2. In this metaphor, circle the word(s) that identify the vehicle

   a. Life is going to be *clear sailing* from now on.

3. Which has greater power? (Circle)   Target   *Vehicle*

4. Which gains the greater benefit? (Circle)   *Target*   Vehicle

5. In this metaphor, circle the word that implies the attribute of the horses.

   a. The young boy's *strength* was like that of a thousand pulling horses as he lifted the car off of his mother.

6. Which metaphor has structural alignment? (Circle)

   a. That gossipy woman is a star falling from the sky.

   b. *That gossipy woman is a humming bird flitting about from flower to flower.*

CHAPTER 7

Metamining: Deconstructing Metaphors for Meaning

Now there's a look in your eyes, like black holes in the sky.
—Pink Floyd, "Shine On You Crazy Diamond"

The members of the 1970s rock group, Pink Floyd, were masters at developing metaphors in their lyrical content. Their lyrics, even those that are more obscure such as the one above, carry a haunting message that causes us to search deeply for the meaning. And when we find that meaning, we discover the sheer genius of the imagery in their songs. Take a moment to consider this lyric. The song is about Syd Barrett, guitarist and a founding member of Pink Floyd. As a child, he was a very bright and intelligent. Later in life, he began to abuse drugs and eventually his personality bordered on schizophrenia. These lyrics describe how his eyes had lost their luster and had become dark like looking into eternity and seeing nothing. It is a sad song but one that illustrates the incredible dark, poetic caricature that was Syd's life. Many who have heard this song looked into the darkness of eternity, were horrified by what they saw, and reversed course to change their lives for the better.

Seeking meaning in life is key to succeeding in life. Words and how they are structured give us a way to understand life's meaning. In particular, metaphors paint meaningful pictures that, if correctly understood, can present powerful elements that inform our knowledge of ourselves and the world around us. "Metamining" is the act of searching for meaning in the elements of the metaphor. Taken as a whole, the metaphor has meaning only in so far as the viewer of the metaphor is able to bring meaning to it. He or she will view the metaphor in its context and apply meaning based upon their perspective influenced by such things as bias, experience, and gender. That, however, does not preclude the fact that a metaphor can be understood and be given meaning. For the purposes of metaformation, this is our goal, but before this can be established, metaphors must first be "mined" for greater meaning.

Metaphors, by their very existence, are meant to bring meaning to an illustration in a simple way. Without this, metaphors have no value except in presentation, to show two things side by side. Presentation is not enough, however, to gain meaning from a metaphor requires us to take apart the metaphor and view its components separately in order to seek greater insight.

Looking Beyond Context

While context of the metaphor has value, unfortunately, it can also limit meaning. The process of metamining motivates one to look beyond the context for added value. It also allows for peripheral but connected concepts to be considered. For example, in my initial application using the metaphor of playing cards, I was able to include everything related to card games, rules, hierarchy, sequence, structures, and players. These added elements of richness helped to define context. Although I have bias, it was recognizable and understood by you, the reader. Although we may not always agree with every perspective brought forth by the originator of a metaphor, we can usually understand it. In this way, the metaphor has served its purpose.

Understandability is only effective, however, if the persons initiating the use of a metaphor explain clearly their approach to the metaphor and how they view the elements and the overall meaning. This should include the meaning of any peripheral concepts as well. However, as you'll recall from the previous chapter, the first thing that must occur is to find a metaphor that is structurally aligned.

Relationship Is Critical

For structural alignment to exist, a relationship must be demonstrated between the target, its attribute or attributes, and the vehicle. One way to begin a search for an appropriate metaphor is to identify the target object and the attributes that you would like to emphasize. Let's look at the following example.

Again, using the metaphor, "The young boy's strength was that of a thousand pulling horses as he lifted the car off of his mother," we've identified the target, the young boy and the attribute, his strength. Next we categorize things that exemplify the attribute of strength and the vehicles that fall into this category. The vehicle is chosen because it is a member of the category that exemplifies the category's defining features. Horses are generally considered strong animals. We could have used a powerful locomotive, a WWF wrestler, or even an ant carrying a hundred times its weight. Each of these objects retains the attribute of strength. However, we chose a thousand pulling horses because of the mental picture magnified by the significant number of horses.

Going back to the metaphor of playing cards, we are now better prepared to understand the power of that metaphor. Playing cards and living life have a relational structural alignment in that, to some degree, both are seen as games of chance. We might have used the attribute of "chance" and chosen horse racing, Russian roulette, or any other activity that involves chance. However, multiple attributes were included such as the fact that cards have hierarchical values or priorities, as does life. Most card games allow one to draw additional cards while discarding others, just as life includes decisions and their consequences. Finally, in the same way that card games have rules, so does living life.

Attributes Point to Principles

When one digs deeper into the game of cards, new insights begin to reveal themselves. At this point, principles can be derived from the metaphor. Incredible power begins to emerge in the ability of the vehicle to inform the target of additional benefits it brings to the relationship. Consider the following:

- Playing a winning hand requires one to keep victory in their sights.
- When you are failing let your playing experience and your instincts, take over.

- Stay focused on all the cards that are being played and the sequence of play.
- Reject distractions.
- Teams provide more cards at your disposal to increase your chances of winning.
- There are champions on every team – use them.
- A team member can be an asset.

The following Table 7.1 more clearly shows the initial attributes as well as these just listed for a total of ten. The table also shows the principles that emerged and were stated in the first chapter.

Table 7.1. Attributes to Principles

Attributes given by the vehicle (Playing cards)	The attributes point to these guiding principles
Cards held by each player are driven by chance and play the hand you've been dealt.	Work with what you have in life.
Most cards games allow one to draw additional cards while discarding others.	You will always have more chances to improve your situation.
Card games have rules that must be followed.	Learn the rules of the game of life.
Playing a winning hand requires one to keep victory in their sights.	Envision yourself succeeding.
When you are failing let your playing experience and your instincts take over.	When you lack vision follow your instincts.
Stay focused on all the cards that are being played and the sequence.	Focus can clarify your vision and timing.
Reject distractions.	Stop trying to multi-task.
Teams provide more cards at your disposal to increase your changes of winning.	You don't have to go through life alone. Strengthen your productivity and decision-making through teamwork.
There are champions on every team – use them.	Key team members can help you achieve your vision or that of your organization.
A team member can be an asset.	Recognize good colleagues when they cross your path.

Translating Attributes

The translation of attributes to principles is somewhat of an art that most of us can develop. While the process is the same for everyone, the outcomes may be uniquely different. This is because attributes may have different meanings for different people. These meanings will be impacted by previous experiences. If one has never played cards, then the attributes will be less than clear and certainly the principles will not be readily understood.

Attributes and emerging principles will be affected by bias. If one has only played solitaire, the attributes involving teamwork may not be readily apparent. However, that does not mean that another metaphor can't be developed using an alternate vehicle in the same category.

Past experiences can cloud the understanding of vehicles that exhibit attributes representing good or evil, which can skew the principles that emerge. Finally, attributes evoke emotions, which vary with individuals in type and degree of intensity. In situations where these issues may exist, it may be better for us to stick to more common, well-known, metaphors that minimize the chance of being misunderstood.

Learning Reinforcement Exercise

1. Circle the two things being compared in each sentence, and tell how they are alike.

    a. The manufacturer's rep is a bulldog.

    _____

    _____

    _____

    b. Our production line slowed down like a ship creeping into the harbor at night.

    _____

    _____

    _____

2. Consider the following examples of the metamining process. Fill in the empty cells for the second and third example.

Metaphor	Target	Attribute	Category	Vehicle	Principle
Life is like playing cards.	Life	Card games have rules that must be followed.	Things with rules.	Playing cards	Learn the rules of the game of life.
He is slow as molasses.	He		Things that are slow.		Being slow is not an admired trait.
The girl ran like the wind.					

Answers: Answers are in italics

1. Circle the two things being compared in each sentence, and tell how they are alike.
   a. The *manufacturer's rep* is a *bulldog.*
      The bulldog is strong and forceful as is the manufacturer's rep.
   b. Our production line slowed down like a ship creeping into the harbor at night.
      Ships must enter the harbor slowly, especially at night when visibility is bad. The production line was slowed to a crawl.

2. Consider the following examples of the metamining process. Fill in the empty blocks for the second and third example.

Metaphor	Target	Attribute	Category	Vehicle	Principle
Life is like playing cards.	Life	Card games have rules that must be followed.	Things with rules.	playing cards	Learn the rules of the game of life.
He is slow as molasses.	He	*Slowness*	Things that are slow.	*molasses*	Being slow is not an admired trait.
The girl ran like the wind.	*girl*	*Speed*	*Things that go fast.*	*wind*	*Being quick is an admired trait.*

CHAPTER 8

Metaforming: Reconstructing Metaphors

And if a mental picture's all I've got, to go on
For a while or more
Girl you know I'll always think of you, think of you
Yes if a mental picture's all I've got, to go on, I know
You're a picture to remember.
                    —Jon Secada, Words and Music, 1994

Putting a metaphor together is what I call metaforming. It is a creative process, which involves reconstructing the elements of the metaphor in such a way that it makes sense and creates a mental image that is easily understood. This is what I call "Picturesquing"—the "act" of creating a mental image that evokes some emotional response. The response could be shock, joy, fear, or any number of appropriate responses. Picturesquing is an activity that requires the metaformer, the leader, to mentally assemble the metaphor in such a way that the attributes provided by the vehicle are believable and provide the needed value to the target. "The puppy fought off the coyote like a ferocious lion." The picture here is of a lion with its hair up on end, claws slashing about, and sharp teeth snapping. The target, which is the puppy, receives these attributes that takes it from implied puppy cuteness to that of a roaring lion. You could replace the lion with the image of a cornered cat: "The puppy fought off the coyote like a cornered cat." Although this is an appropriate metaphor, it does not carry with it the image of conquering greatness.

Now, let's consider some leadership metaphors. "The leader is a blade of grass." At first it would seem this is a metaphor with very little substance; however, let's picturesque this to gain a better understanding of the image that it is projecting. We have to ask ourselves, "What is the attribute or attributes that are implied by the leader?" A blade of grass is flexible; it bends with the wind. It is growing among other blades of grass. It has roots that nourish it. It can spring back after being walked on. Can you see the leadership attributes implied here? Flexibility, growth, leadership, and the ability to bounce back after a setback are seen as critical attributes for leaders. We can picture the blade of grass that is seemingly insignificant, standing tall but flexing in the wind, bouncing back after being trampled upon and continuing to grow after this kind of abuse.

Transcendenting

One critical aspect of metaforming is *transcendenting*. This is the act of bringing the metaphor into current reality. It is drawing upon the image of the attributes and comparing them with the target to see if they are within the limits of possible experience or knowledge. In other words, does the picture represent the possible? Is it believable?

In the previous example, although we would never accept a literal translation of the leader as a blade of grass, the metaphor makes sense when the visual image is magnified by the comparison of the attributes of flexibility, growth, and resilience. It is within the realm of possibility insofar as it characterizes attributes of a good leader. We are able to bring the metaphor into our current reality by considering the transcendent nature of the comparison between the leader and the blade of grass.

Priming

Another metaforming act is that of "priming." This is the act of creating a benchmark through the use of a metaphor that exemplifies the very best or very worst of something. Metaphors by their very nature are meant to move us to the limits of comparison so that our minds are stretched to include the possibility of a new way of looking at something. Consider, "Leaders are lamps." At first this would seem ludicrous. What does it mean, "Leaders are lamps?" It would seem that this is far outside the realm of possibility. However, on closer examination we know that lamps typically have a shade that softens the glow as leaders must sometimes soften their approach to leading others when circumstances dictate. Lamps are turned off and on just as leaders move to action based upon external forces. Lamps are usually placed at the edges or corners of a room only to be seen or used in times of darkness. Leaders are effective when they allow others to function and only when needed do they bring leadership to the situation. Finally, lamps come in different shapes and sizes just as leaders come from all races, genders, walks of life, and physically different from each other.

What about, "Leaders are pudding." Well, now we have a comparison that would be difficult to defend as within the realm of possibility. Pudding is usually served cold. It is eaten with a spoon. Good pudding doesn't have lumps unless it is a tapioca pudding. It is very difficult to see the possibilities here. There is no benchmark or priming in the comparison of leaders and pudding. No one would get a sense that becoming a leader is of any value. They would not be motivated to follow this kind of leader, nor would they see the need to be led.

Emotive Force

Good metaphors have behind them "emotive force." This means they are able to reach into our basket of emotions and draw out a response that causes us to laugh, cry, sigh, exclaim, and become filled with excitement. When we are confronted with a metaphor that causes us to respond in this way, a memorable event takes place. We are more likely to remember a metaphor that has an emotional response tied to it. This metaphor is said to have emotive force. Consider, "Leaders are elephants circling the pack and protecting the young." This metaphor uses the attributes of leaders as protectors, bold, wise, and watching for intruders. The emotions or emotive force that we sense is that of calm, safety, and protection.

However, consider, "Leaders are cotton candy." The attribute that is implied here is that cotton candy is soft and sweet. Although it is in the realm of possibility for a leader, it does not evoke an emotional response unless you include that of disgust. Emotive force is a critical element in metaforming. It is what gives metaphors strength, memorability, and makes the comparison interesting. These metaphors keep our attention.

Zipping

Metaphors that are too complicated lose their ability to be effective. Including too many attributes or using vehicles that are too complex creates a sense of mental gymnastics in the mind of the listener. The concepts come too quickly and are too dense to properly interpret and therefore become ineffective. Leaders who complicate their message in this way stand to lose the attention of their followers. They get lost in the message and lose focus for the vision.

I use the term "zipping" to refer to the process of bringing the complicated down to understandable terms. This is a primary function of metaphors. They should always make something that is complicated easy to understand through the process of zipping and should also make them easy to remember through engaging emotive force.

As you've probably already guessed, zipping is taken from the act of downloading a large computer file that has been compressed into a zipped file to reduce downloading speed and storage space. It contains all the elements of the original file but without the complications related to size. When the file is opened later, everything is there ready to be used, manipulated, or deleted.

Consider the metaphor, "Leaders are metaphysics." First of all, metaphysics could never be explained without some expanding remarks addressing specific attributes. Secondly, metaphysics lacks emotive force and therefore is not memorable. A zipped file of metaphysics would be simply too large to mentally digest and would lose the interest of the listener.

Now consider the metaphor, "Leaders are a box of assorted chocolates." Assorted chocolates presented in a box contain many attributes but the attributes are not so complex that the idea is lost. Chocolates are placed in individual tray indentations just as leaders each have their place in their organization. Assorted chocolates are different, representing that leaders come in different shapes and sizes. Assorted chocolates also have an emotive force in that we typically get excited when trying to choose our favorite chocolate from the assortment. There is also a sense of anticipation with that first bite. Excitement and anticipation are emotions that most leaders hope their followers feel when they carry out the vision of the organization.

Metalating

Transcending language and cultural barriers are significant hurdles for leaders who must communicate outside of their first language. I call this activity, "metalating." Metalating means forming metaphors that are understood in the language being spoken or the culture that one is relating to. The act of metalating is difficult at best. It requires fluency in the language being spoken and an in-depth understanding of the culture.

Within cultures there are many subcultures wherein a particular metaphor would be highly effective with one group but be offensive with another. It is not my intent to go much further into this but only to say that if one must lead in a second language, it would behoove the leader to be careful with the use of metaphors.

Snapshooting

Sometimes less is better. Metaphors that can be conveyed in just a few words can have significantly greater impact than if they are long and drawn out. I call this "snapshooting." Simplicity can magnify the emotive force of a metaphor by causing the listener to focus on the key attribute being conveyed. Consider this metaphor, "Leaders are thunderstorms." This metaphor has several levels of attributes but the sense is not lost in them. Thunderstorms can come on quick and explosive much like leaders who need to act in emergent situations. Thunderstorms bring needed relief in the form of rain much like leaders who bring relief through inspiring, encouraging, and building up the faith of followers. After the thunderstorm there is usually a time of calm and reflection much like there is when a leader and his or her followers have overcome their challenges. All of these images are conveyed in the metaphor of a thunderstorm. The listener gets a snapshot of what is meant to be conveyed about leaders. It is clear and compact and has emotive force and brevity.

Learning Reinforcement Exercise

Draw an arrow from the title to its correct definition:

Title	Definition
Picturesquing	The act of bringing the metaphor into current reality.
Transcendenting	The ability to reach into our basket of emotions and draw out a response.
Priming	The forming of metaphors that are understood in the language being spoken or the culture that you are relating to.
Emotive force	The ability to convey something in just a few words, which can have significantly greater impact than long and drawn out expressions.
Zipping	The "act" of creating a mental image that evokes some emotional response.
Metalating	The process of bringing the complicated down to understandable terms.
Snapshooting	The act of creating a benchmark through the use of a metaphor that exemplifies the very best or very worst of something.

Answers:

Title	Definition
Picturesquing	The act of bringing the metaphor into current reality.
Transcendenting	The ability to reach into our basket of emotions and draw out a response.
Priming	The forming of metaphors that are understood in the language being spoken or the culture that you are relating to.
Emotive force	The ability to convey something in just a few words, which can have significantly greater impact than long and drawn out expressions.
Zipping	The "act" of creating a mental image that evokes some emotional response.
Metalating	The process of bringing the complicated down to understandable terms.
Snapshooting	The act of creating a benchmark through the use of a metaphor that exemplifies the very best or very worst of something.

CHAPTER 9

Searching for a New Metaphor

Like a Rolling Stone
　—Bob Dylan

Jason knew that the company was a reflection of him and wondered whether the current attributes could describe who he had become as well? As tempting as it was, however, he didn't have time to think about that for the moment. Jason's old partner, Dillon, had long since cashed out and was living somewhere in the south of France. Lucky guy. He thought briefly about those days in the Irish pub and the fun they had while envisioning what their organization could become. It was certainly not the organization that had emerged.

The vision had been built on the metaphor of fast cars, Porsches in particular. Jason had always been a Porsche fan; no, a Porsche enthusiast would be more accurate. He loved everything about the shape, sound, and engineering excellence that they represented. He wanted the company to emulate everything that Porsche stood for; however, that was no longer possible. He also realized that the company needed him to lead again. He needed to fill everyone up and get them to rev their engines again. They needed to get back on the starting line, but the metaphor was worn out and broken down. Jason decided to take a walk and clear his head.

Los Angeles can be a beautiful town, full of excitement and interesting people. He turned the corner down Sunset Drive and looked to where the old Tower Records used to be just a few years earlier. It was great back in the good old days, the days of vinyl, hair down to their waists, and parties into the early morning. Now, they all wore their hair neatly trimmed, and dressed in tailored Armani suits. He longed for those old jeans that he wore hitchhiking across country that had patches all over them. He especially loved the little harmonica pocket that was sewn on by that girl in Albuquerque. He would tuck the "C" harp into its little pouch and pull it out whenever he heard someone strumming a guitar. It was a glorious time, carefree, full of adventure and no responsibilities. Now he had responsibility over a multimillion dollar budget, 150 plus artists and musicians, and a staff of over 300. It made him tired just thinking about it.

As he walked, he saw some kids playing the old game of 4-Square. Remember that? You would use chalk to draw out four squares that were large enough for you to stand in and you and three friends would each take a square while bouncing the ball back and forth between you. The ball was allowed to bounce only once in your square before you had to bounce it to someone else. Seeing them reminded him of the joy and simplicity of being a kid.

Later, he started to think about his company again and couldn't shake the thought of the game of 4-Square being played by those kids. When he returned to the office from his walk, he went back to working on the responses from his staff. His staff had listed current attributes, and he had made a list of polar opposites. Then he thought, "What things would best represent the new attributes?" He made the following short list of categories that he thought would easily contain things that would be a good fit for a new metaphor.

Current attributes	New attributes (Polar opposites)	Categories
Lethargic	Energetic	Sports
Unfocused	Focused	Games
Too big	Right size	Animals
Not motivating	Motivated	Cars
No more joy	Full of Joy	
Bureaucratic	Flexible	
Indecisive	Decisive	
Bound up	Free	
Too safe	Resilient	

As he considered each category and some things in each category, he settled on sports. He could have used cars again, but the Porsche metaphor was for a different time, and they needed something new and fresh.

Jason's mind kept drifting back to the game of 4-Square. What was it that was so intriguing? Was it the action of four people hitting something back and forth between them? Was it the quick reflex responses that it took to recognize the ball coming at you and then batting it into someone else's square? Was it the ball? Then it hit him! That's it; he wanted their company to be like a ball! Pure inspiration took over in that moment. It was like when you hear a great hook in a song. It stays with you. You can't seem to get it out of your mind. You play it over and over again in your thoughts. You hum it under your breath. As simple as that sounds, he realized that he had stumbled on what might be their new metaphor.

As he thought about it, he realized that something as simple as a ball had hidden attributes that he could tap into to help define a new vision for the company. It could also help shape the way they would redefine their mission and handle challenges in the future. He set about trying to discover those hidden attributes. Having studied linguistics and cognitive behavior in college, he knew that metaphors were a comparison between two things that were similar in relationship but not necessarily in strength. Although his company was strong, the ball represented attributes that seemed consistent with the new attributes that they desired to represent. However, first he needed to make sure he was comparing two things that could rationally be compared. He had to look at their structures.

Structural Alignment of the Metaphor

Jason considered whether the company and the ball were structurally similar. The company and the ball both had boundaries. The people in the company could be seen like molecules that make up the ball. The values, vision, and mission held the company together. However, these elements had eroded over time and the people were gradually drifting apart from each other, causing a breakdown in the organizational structure. They needed to tap into the power of a new metaphor in order to bring everyone back together as a team.

Jason knew that if the ball turned out to be the new metaphor, researching the metaphor was only part of the plan. He would need to articulate a new leadership approach utilizing the metaphor to color his language and bring understanding and clarity to his delivery. He would also need to be consistent in the use of the metaphor in order to weave it into the fabric of the company from their values, to the vision, through the mission statement, and down into their goals and objectives. Everything would have to line up, but first he needed to think through the ball metaphor more deeply.

Balls can be made from many things. Some are rubber, some are plastic, some are made from wood, and some are made from glass and very fragile. The size and shape of the ball used in the metaphor would need to be considered. Most balls are round, but the football is oblong. This creates its own dynamics. How balls are thrown impacts the trajectory and, therefore, the distance the ball will travel. Oblong balls such as a football don't bounce in a predictable manner. He also knew that he couldn't decide on a metaphor without input from his colleagues. That afternoon he sent an e-mail to his Executive Team to meet the next morning. They needed to address this issue while they had a chance.

Getting Others Involved

Everyone attended the meeting this time. Apparently, the word had gotten out that the boss was on a rampage. Well, whatever the reason, it was great to get everyone in the same room to toss some ideas around. Jason knew that some of the folks gathered did not have a bent toward creativity. It's funny that they ended up in this business and loved it. Without mentioning a metaphor, Jason began the meeting by asking everyone to write down the polar opposites of their original list of current attributes. Although he didn't show them his list, theirs corresponded with his.

He then asked them to write down categories that might hold things that would characterize the new list of polar opposites of attributes. Their list was longer but included the three that he had written in the solitude of his office. The exercise was confirming the process that they were using was logical and rational. He took note of the comments and dismissed the team. They looked at each other wondering if Jason was out of his mind. He knew they were expecting something else but he was not going to give anyone a tongue-lashing. He was on a mission to discover a new metaphor.

In the category of balls, there are many types as stated earlier. Jason needed a particular type of ball that exhibited similar attributes to the new attributes they had come up with. Basketballs are too cumbersome and require significant skill to maneuver effectively. Footballs were out of the question because of their odd shape and aerodynamic properties. Baseballs were easy to throw but too hard. Tennis balls, on the other hand, were fun, the right size for throwing, bounced well, were flexible, and resilient. They have a soft outer skin that has a texture that is comfortable, and they come in fun neon colors. They are the right consistency and contain a lot of kinetic energy that can be transferred into a trajectory of long distance. When they hit a wall, they bounce off without permanently changing shape. They offer attributes of resilience and agility. They can be used aggressively without really hurting anyone and therefore risky behavior with tennis balls can be tolerated. They had their metaphor, a tennis ball. However, as he thought about the ball, he couldn't help but see that the game of tennis also had a couple of other great attributes: (1) You must keep your eyes on the ball and (2) you should stay on the balls of your feet to remain maneuverable and light so that you can change direction immediately.

Translating the Attributes into Principles

That night Jason couldn't sleep very well. The metaphor continued to roll around in his head. He was anxious to put more thoughts down on paper. However, he was concerned about how to share this new metaphor. He had to construct the metaphor in language that made sense to others. It needed to inspire, give direction, provide boundaries, and establish how they would work together in the future. Although a tennis ball might at first seem like a simple object, he knew there was still much more to learn about it and how it could inform their culture and mission. He also knew that their branding was suffering. This was a primary result of their lack of focus. Perhaps the metaphor could help there as well?

He got to the office early the next morning. The cleaning people were just finishing up. Bill, the cleaning company supervisor, greeted him with a surprise smile and handshake. They had known each other for many years but it had been a long time since Jason had come in this early, having, for the past several years, resorted to taking a daily morning stroll on the beach before coming to work. It was good to see Bill. He reminded Jason of happier days.

Things were tough back then but his team was tougher. They were hungry to get their piece of the pie. Jason asked Bill about his family. His wife worked with him but was cleaning on another floor. Bill's son had gone off to grad school at the University of Edinburgh, and his daughter was studying Forensic Psychology at USC. "How he could afford this?" Jason thought. He didn't understand, but Bill was clearly proud of them and rightfully so.

Jason stopped and got a cup of coffee from the employee kitchen, black this morning and strong and slipped into his office. Setting up coffee on a timer every evening before he left work always assured that he'd have a good hot cup of coffee when he returned the next morning. Jason suspected that others in the office appreciated coming in to a hot pot of coffee as well. He made a habit of setting the timer an hour earlier than he usually arrived just in case he came in early as he did this morning. Jason turned on his computer and waited for it to boot up.

After quickly scanning his e-mails, he did a Google search on "How to make tennis balls." His screen quickly filled with YouTube videos, articles, and websites all dedicated to telling and showing how to make tennis balls. Apparently others were interested in tennis balls as well. "This was weird," he thought. The first pdf document that he opened spelled out the entire process.

Large rubber sheets are slid into a machine that stamps out rubber slugs. Jason was reminded how most of his team came to his company directly out of college having received their stamp of approval to enter the workforce. Still green, they were the raw material that he had built into successful music executives. The rubber slugs are melted and poured into molds in the shape of half-shells. Then these are fed into a machine that shakes them until they are all facing the same direction with the open side up. The picture he saw here was that each new employee had to learn the rules of the game and develop some core competencies. Then, the half-shells are dropped into trays where glue is applied to the rims. They go into a press, and another set of half-shells are turned upside down and pressed against these. The press closes, squeezing the two sides together and forming a perfect ball. The press also regulates the pressure of the air inside the ball. Apparently, there are strict regulations about the pressure because it determines how much bounce a tennis ball requires in order to satisfy the regulations. He needed to make sure his employees could handle the pressure of the music business so that they would be able to bounce back after a setback.

When the balls come out of the press, the end result is called a tennis ball core. The cores are then sent on to a machine that scuffs up the surface of the ball. Having a rougher surface allows glue to stick better. After his employees develop their core competencies, they hit the streets and get roughed up a bit as they learn how to swim with the sharks. Meanwhile, felt is cut to wrap around the ball. The felt is cut into peanut-shaped strips. When two of these strips are wrapped together around the core, they link up perfectly and there are no overlapping or empty spots. He did his best to help his employees weather this period of indoctrination by encouraging them, assigning mentors, and teaching them the ropes.

At this point neon green or another bright colored felt is used to increase visibility. Tennis balls can be found in many different colors, much like the diversity he had in his company. The balls then go through a machine that rolls them around and presses them, making sure that the felt is securely attached to all surfaces of the ball. At some point in the indoctrination process, when they think the employee is ready to represent artists, they take them through a panel interview to see what they've learned and to make sure they are ready to get in the game. The balls are then lined up and stamped or printed with a logo of the company that is manufacturing them. His employees are finally issued business cards that become their stamp of approval.

The balls are then dropped into cans, and the cans are sealed and pressurized. The reason that cans are pressurized is to maintain a specific pressure on the inside of the balls. This is why you hear that whoosh of air rushing out when you open up a new can. He makes every effort to keep his employees on their game by allowing just enough competition to keep the pressure on them to remain fresh and up to date on new artists, projects, and marketing strategies.

Jason discovered some very interesting facts about how tennis balls are made and how the process related to how they trained and prepared their young college grads to navigate the murky waters of the music industry. He then had to consider several issues. Was the metaphor applicable in a very real sense? Could it withstand the scrutiny of application in their present reality? Could the metaphor evoke an emotional response using terminology that would illustrate the attributes expressed by his Executive Team? Finally, could he articulate the metaphor in words that are concise without losing the meanings embedded in the metaphor? At this point, he had to take the new attributes and translate them into principles that would guide the company into the future. Below he added the list that characterized the new attributes and the corresponding principles. He removed the list of categories since he had settled on the game of tennis and the tennis ball.

Current attributes	New attributes (Polar opposites)	Guiding principles
Lethargic	Energetic	Do things that inject energy into the daily life of the organization.
Unfocused	Focused	Stay focused on the vision.
Too big	Right size	Be willing to become the size of organization that you want, not what others say you should become.
Not motivating	Motivated	Find ways to keep everyone motivated at all times.
No more joy	Full of Joy	Make sure to maintain a joyful workplace culture.
Bureaucratic	Flexible	Design an organizational structure that can flex with the times and situations.
Indecisive	Decisive	Make sure the decision making process is not cumbersome.
Bound up	Free	Be willing to take risks.
Too safe	Resilient	Don't take life too seriously, and always look to the good in every outcome.

Jason pondered these principles throughout the day as he had opportunity. Nothing had changed since their meeting the day prior, however, everyone seemed to be in a posture of, "What next?" He thought about their vision statement first, "To be an international force in music that would change the lives of everyone who heard or saw the incredible mix of sound or visual performance by our artists and productions." This was a good vision statement but lacked movement or motion. The new metaphor would need to propel the company on a new trajectory. He could see how the tennis ball metaphor would work well here.

Then he considered their mission statement. Unfortunately, it had been a long time since he'd read it, and he was unable to remember it word for word. He finally found a copy, "Our mission is to make international stars of our artists by producing and promoting their work around the world to audiences of every class, race, and ethnic group." Wow, this sure sounded good. He wasn't sure how the metaphor might alter the mission statement though.

Their values seemed sound. They rested on the acronym of TRUTH; Trust, Reflection, Uniqueness, Teamwork, and Humility. Several of their values had eroded over time and would probably need revisiting as to how they could maintain consistency with their values in their daily business activities. They had a long way to go to reengineer his company to meet the adjectives and attributes that he wanted this company to reflect.

Jason called another meeting with his Executive Team for the following week. He planned to unveil the potential new metaphor and ask for feedback. At this point, he needed to beta-test the metaphor for acceptance and emotional response.

The meeting went well with a majority of the Executive Team recognizing the need for a new metaphor and seeing how the tennis ball could easily fit what they were looking for. However, they were still a bit skeptical as to how they could incorporate the principles and articulate them to the rest of the company. They began working on rewriting the vision and mission statements.

Questions to Consider

1. What three current attributes or adjectives would you use to describe the current condition of your organization?
2. What are the polar opposite of these attributes?
3. Can you identify guiding principles that would adequately describe these polar opposites?

PART 4

Combining and Communicating, and Applying New Metaphors

CHAPTER 10

Ligering: Combining and Creating New Metaphors

The World is a Vampire.
— Smashing Pumpkins, "Bullet with Butterfly Wings"

Sometimes one metaphor is incapable of adequately providing all the elements needed to be effective. In this instance you can consider combining two metaphors. One of the funniest combinations that I had ever heard came from the movie, *Napoleon Dynamite*. Napoleon, a clumsy, nerdy, high school student, is quite an artist (snicker), and in one scene he is sitting on the steps of his high school sketching something. His girlfriend steps out of the doors of the school and takes a couple of steps down and sits behind and to the right of Napoleon. She asks him what he is drawing? He responds, "A liger, pretty much my favorite animal. It's like a lion and tiger mixed, bred for its skills and magic." I'm not sure how he determined the attributes but clearly, he was convinced of the liger's ability to live up to them.

This is a great illustration of combining metaphors to come up with something that captures the attributes of two vehicles. In this case the lion and the tiger. It could have been a lion and a baboon, called a "liboon," or a "babion." It could be an animal that is very strong and majestic as well as nimble and steals like a thief. I don't know in what case you would apply the metaphor of a liboon but you can see that combining metaphors or, "ligering" as I call it, is not a difficult thing to do.

Ligered metaphors don't need to be from similar categories. In the illustration I took two animals and combined them into a metaphor, a liboon. But what about ligering animate and inanimate objects? What if you were to combine an elephant and a tank for example? You would come up with a metaphor that had the following attributes: (1) powerful,

(2) protective, (3) able to move through any terrain, (4) tough skinned, (5) able to block opposition, (6) obedient, (7) impervious to pain, and (8) able to work long hours. You could call this an "elephank." I don't know about you, but I'd love to hire someone like this.

Another way that metaphors can be used in the creative process is when you combine them to come up with something new or unique. What about combining a robot and a human arm? Robotic Arm. Hmm, seems like someone has already come up with that. Combining or innovating in this way can help you create new products and technologies.

Humans have a natural tendency to want to combine their human attributes with inanimate objects. A case in point is the talking car from the 1982 hit television series, *Night-Rider*, starring David Hasselhoff as Michael Knight. We see other examples of this in films like the *Terminator* series. Still another example is the combination of the computer and television to produce the smartphone. We can go on and on with examples of how metaphors have been used to create real or fictional things with unique attributes. However, it is important to make sure that you test your metaphor so that it reflects the attributes you desire, and that others see the reflection accurately as well.

Metaphor Construction

Just as in building construction, you need to use sound methods to construct metaphors. Unless your foundation is strong, the entire metaphor is weak and will eventually fail to produce the power you need to move your organization forward. Consider if your home were built with cement blocks on a foundation of toothpicks. Eventually, and very quickly, the foundation would collapse.

Choosing the right attributes that you hope the metaphor will project is the first step that takes place in the metaframing stage. As you decide on the attributes you want to project, you create categories of things that exemplify those attributes. After you create lists within these categories, you begin to look for things that are the best fit and have the most direct structural relationship with the target.

In the story, the target was the record company and is the thing that gains added value from the vehicle, or the tennis ball. The metaphor would be something like, "The company (target) is a tennis ball (vehicle)." The vehicle points back to the target those qualities that exemplify the attributes the target wishes to project. Hence, the attributes of the tennis ball point back to the company, and the company gains the added value of these attributes. The attributes are now attributable to the company. The company owns the attributes and begins to project them. These are the first steps in ensuring that sound reconstruction methods are being employed.

In most metaforming exercises, the target is looking for a vehicle that can produce action. The metaphor, "The Volkswagen is a jar of honey," would not gain any action or activity from the use of a jar of honey as the vehicle. However, if the metaphor were something like, "The Volkswagen is an F-16 fighter jet," it would definitely project back to the Volkswagen the attribute of speed. You can picture the Volkswagen flying along at supersonic speed. This is what I earlier called, "picturesquing."

When combining targets and metaphors to create new metaphors it can be helpful to combine the vehicle and target words to create new words. I illustrated this in the example of the liger and the elephank. This creates simplicity that others can easily see and understand the combined attributes that you are trying to project. This, as you'll remember is called "snapshooting."

Questions to Consider

1. What metaphor adequately describes your current or past organization?
2. What is the target and vehicle of this metaphor?
3. What new metaphor describes what you would like this organization to become?

CHAPTER 11

Communicating Your New Metaphor

The most important thing in communication is hearing what isn't said.
—Peter Drucker

As I mentioned in the introduction, this book was written for leaders or those aspiring to be leaders. The main function of leadership is to communicate and inspire followers. This is no easy task. There are many books written about leadership communication but none that I've seen talk about or understand the power of using metaphors for strategizing, planning, branding, and communicating a new direction for an organization.

Metaphors, if chosen correctly, have the potential to inject new energy into organizations in ways no other tool or method can. Metaphors are self-explanatory; they are simple; they communicate a lot in a compact way; they add action; they describe ways to respond to the environment and challenges; they can identify new products and services; and they define ways to achieve goals and objectives. Metaphors can be the saving grace for an organization and its leaders if the process is followed correctly and these new metaphors are applied in a systematic manner.

See Your Metaphor

Metaphors house their power in the form of mental images. Visual representations are some of the most powerful ways to convey ideas. Remember the saying, "A picture is worth a thousand words?" It is possible to capture numerous ideas and concepts in the form of a picture. The interpretation, however, can be varied particularly if it is an abstract picture. That is why I always recommend metaphors that contain vehicles that are easy to understand.

When you've chosen a metaphor and taken the time to metamine or deconstruct it, you will have discovered many layers of attributes and concepts that will require you to choose which ones you want to apply to your target. As you consider these chosen attributes, it is important to think deeply about them so that you can gain as much understanding and as much power from the metaphor as possible. Let's consider the metaphor, "Our organization will fly with the eagles." The target is "organization" and the vehicle is "eagles." The word "fly" is a modifier that helps us understand what aspect of the eagles is the most important one in terms of the metaphor. As you start to "picturesque" the mental image of flying with the eagles you may come across some of the following visual impressions:

1. Eagles tend to fly alone.
2. If you were able to ride the back of an eagle, you might see their eyes scanning to and fro hunting for game, looking for potential predators (although there are few in the air), wings outstretched and supported by prevailing wind streams.
3. Their feathers are smoothed back, white on the head, trailing back to the wings, and white tail.
4. They are majestic, with sharp, clear eyes.
5. They are confident flyers and have a posture of confidence.
6. When they see prey, they swoop down with claws outstretched ready to grab.
7. After they grab their prey, they immediately begin to flap their powerful wings and begin a sharp climb into the heavens and back to their nest.
8. Their wing and chest muscles are prominent, which depicts great strength.
9. They cast a magnificent shadow as they pass overhead.
10. Perched eagles seem calm, self-assured, and aware.

You can see, there are many visual representations that can be derived from the mental pictures of a flying eagle. Let's take the same mental images and see how you might picture the vision of the organization:

1. Eagles tend to fly alone; *the organization is alone in the industry sector in which it competes.*

2. If you were able to ride the back of an eagle, you might see their eyes scanning to and fro hunting for game, looking for potential predators (although there are few in the air), wings outstretched, and supported by prevailing wind streams; *as the organization depicts a constant awareness of the competitive climate, riding the course of product demand with its core competencies carrying them.*

3. Their feathers are smoothed back, white on the head, and trailing back to the wings and white tail; *as the organizational structure is balanced and beautiful, the culture is not easily ruffled.*

4. They are majestic, with sharp, clear eyes, *as the vision of the organization is clear, easy to understand, and held in high regard by its employees.*

5. They are confident flyers and have a posture of confidence, *as the organization is confident because it has done its homework. It remains confident in the face of competition.*

6. When they see prey, they swoop down with claws outstretched ready to grab, *as the organization is ready to jump on opportunities and into markets that reveal a demand for its products.*

7. After they grab their prey, they immediately begin to flap their powerful wings and begin a sharp climb into the heavens and back to their nest, *as the organization is quick to provide good service and support from its headquarters.*

8. Their wing and chest muscles are prominent, which depict great strength, *as the organization's branding represents strength.*

9. They cast a magnificent shadow as they pass overhead, *as the organization is easily known in its industry and one that other organizations aspire to be like.*

10. Perched eagles seem calm, self-assured, and aware, *as the organization is settled, organized, and understands the marketplace.*

In each case, it is possible to apply "flying with eagles" to organizational concepts that are easily seen in a mental picture. You must be able to capture the nuances of the picture in order to squeeze out every drop of power the metaphor depicts. This can take time but it can be very rewarding when you discover many layers of comparisons that you can apply to various aspects of the target, in this case the organization. However, seeing the metaphor is not sufficient. You must also conduct yourself in accordance with the metaphor. One way to do this is to prepare your mind each day before you go to work. Take some time in the morning to find a quiet room in your house our somewhere in your backyard or property, and close your eyes and see in your mind the metaphor. Imagine living in the metaphor. In this case, it is an organization; but you are a vital part of that organization and your professional life should emulate the metaphor as well. That is where walking the metaphor comes in.

Walk Your Metaphor

Seeing your metaphor is important and must be done before you can walk out the metaphor in your daily life. You must learn to live within your metaphor. It should become like a comfortable winter coat that protects you from the wind and cold. Just normal walking seems like a fairly simple activity for someone who is physically capable. However, the act of walking requires you to choose a direction, exert energy, lean in the direction of the walk, and put one foot in front of the other. Walking out your metaphor requires similar actions.

Choosing the direction to walk out your metaphor requires a level of commitment, just as does walking. You have to be in a place of total agreement with your metaphor in order to comply with it and choose a direction consistent with the metaphor. This is not a difficult thing since you should have already derived principles from your chosen attributes of the metaphor. These principles become your guiding principles. They define the direction you and your organization will go. At this point, you need to lean into it.

Leaning into the direction to walk out your metaphor requires a shift of weight. You must first commit, then lean or shift your organizational weight, such as your financial resources, in the direction of your metaphor. Your lean can be easily identified by your actions. They demonstrate your commitment and your willingness to follow the direction of the metaphor. However, you must activate your energy to catapult your organization in the direction of the metaphor in order to begin your actual walk.

Your organization has kinetic or stored energy in the motivation and desires of your people. They are your greatest asset and essential to the launch of the new metaphor. Just as it takes an initial push to activate your energy when you walk, you must also activate your energy to launch the new metaphor. When you walk, you rock forward in the direction of your goal by shifting weight into your lean and pushing off the ball of your trailing foot. From an organizational perspective, you must be the first to roll off your current position or current metaphor in the direction of your new metaphor. This can be seen as you take actions in support of the metaphor. If you must get lean, you need to rock off your present size by assessing your workforce and making cuts or reassignments. This action demonstrates your willingness to activate the metaphor. It is your first step in this particular example. All subsequent steps should demonstrate your commitment to your new metaphor. This is walking out your metaphor. In addition to walking it out, you must also talk your metaphor.

Talk Your Metaphor

Introducing your new metaphors to your audience, be it your family, friends, colleagues, or employees, requires you to begin to make use of the metaphor in your daily conversations. This ensures that you have done your homework well, analyzed where your organization is, where it wants to go, and the attributes that will catapult it in the desired direction. Metaphors also affirm your choice of vehicle(s) and can create new conversations with regard to rebranding and new products, processes, and services.

The act of talking requires certain things to happen. You must have some air in your lungs, compress your lungs by beginning to breathe out, think about what you are going to say, use your mouth and lips to shape the words coming out, and control the amount of air by opening or constricting the throat to regulate your volume. When you talk your metaphor, you must take similar actions.

Before you talk your metaphor, be sure you are prepared to talk it. You must understand your metaphor through many levels. You should have taken considerable time metamining or deconstructing your metaphor in order to have a solid understanding of its depth, breadth, and power. This is like having your lungs full of air, ready to talk.

As you begin to exhale, or construct your conversations, you will be connecting your references to your metaphor. This will require you to say it in different ways, referring to it from many different perspectives. It should become the focus of most every conversation in the workplace for you and your leadership team. They should all be talking the metaphor on a regular basis. This may sound odd at first, but as you talk your metaphor on a daily basis it will get easier and easier. We tend to talk most about things we are interested in or things that we know something about. As I mentioned earlier, your metaphor will become like a warm, comfortable winter coat.

The first time you refer to the new metaphor, you may get blank stares unless the person or persons you are talking to have been involved in choosing the metaphor. Although we use metaphors in our daily language every day, we seldom talk about the structure of language and how we put sentences together. It is a natural part of learning a basic language either through imitation or structured training.

As I mentioned earlier, similes and metaphors are related but different. They are like language cousins. They have the same family blood but have distinctions as well. Metaphors carry stronger action and are more effective as a tool for transformation. When you say, "He is an ox," you are saying something much more powerful than, "He is like an ox." Being an ox implies that he has all the characteristics of an ox versus being, "like an ox," which implies he may have some characteristics and may not have others. Depending on whether you use a simile or metaphor will determine the degree of acceptance or confusion you may encounter. This is where you must be clear about what you are implying. Sometimes, you can use a simile in place of the metaphor, particularly if you deliberately want to soften the comparison. Nevertheless, the more you understand and talk your metaphor, the more comfortable you will become with it, and the more ways you will find to express your metaphor.

Learning Reinforcement Exercise

1. Ligering is combining two vehicles into one. One example previously described was that of a lion and a tiger, or liger. Create a different combination based upon an attribute of your choosing.

_____

2. What is the attribute you started with? _____

3. Does the ligering combination that you created represent this attribute?
   Circle: Yes   No

4. The three aspects of communicating your new metaphor are (Circle the best answer):
   a. Seeing your metaphor
   b. Walking your metaphor
   c. Talking your metaphor
   d. All of the above

Numbers 1–3 are of your choosing. The answer for number 4 is italicized:
   1. Ligering is a combining two vehicles into one. One example previously described was that of a lion and a tiger, or liger. Create a different combination based upon an attribute of your choosing.___
   _____

   2. What is the attribute you started with? _____

   3. Does the ligering combination that you created represent this attribute?
      Circle: Yes   No

   4. The three aspects of communicating your new metaphor are:
      a. Seeing your metaphor
      b. Walking your metaphor
      c. Talking your metaphor
      d. *All of the above*

CHAPTER 12

Metaplying: Applying Your Metaphor

You Ain't Nothing but a Hound Dog.
—Elvis

After you have chosen your new metaphor, the first thing you need to look at is the vision statement or vision of the organization. If the vision statement must be rewritten, the new statement should capture the strength, power, or direction of the metaphor. This same process then carries down through the mission statement. After this, the next part of the application process is to see how your new metaphor filters down through your goals and objectives. This is metaplying.

You must ask yourself a number of questions:

- Do your current goals and objectives reflect the attributes that the new metaphor projects?
- Will you have to rethink your goals and objectives, modify them, or completely eliminate them?
- Will you discover new goals and objectives that are consistent with the new metaphor? If so, how do these new goals and objectives impact the overall strategy of your organization? Also, are those who are responsible to carrying out your new or modified goals and objectives equipped to do so?
- Will you have to reassign management or staff to accomplish these objectives so that the metaphor is properly supported?
- Will it require you to restructure your organization so that it is more consistent with the new metaphor? How will this impact budgets, revenues, and costs? Are your facilities sufficient to support production under the new metaphor?

- Will you have to downsize your hard assets or your rolling
  stock?
- Will it require you to modify your current marketing strategy?
- Will it impact whom you do business with? Will your current
  suppliers be able to provide materials and services that they
  were able to under the old system? What about your distributors? Are they sufficiently staffed and connected to get your
  products to the markets you desire?
- Will your target markets change? Will some be added or will
  some be eliminated all together?
- Will you suddenly find yourself able or unable to provide new
  or altered products or services to new market segments?

Application of your new metaphor requires you to understand the principles derived from the attributes of your new metaphor well in order
to compare organizational issues to these principles. Principles are the
guiding forces that help your organization maintain alignment with its
strategy. These principles should, whenever possible, be stated as action
verbs. However, that may not always be possible, particularly when the
principle involves a state of being such as, "We should be generous at
all times." This could be stated as action, "We should give at all times";
however, the meaning is somewhat altered. You should not get too flus-
tered if you run into this since the goal is to develop principles that truly
capture what you are hoping will provide the right guidelines to reflect
your desired outcomes.

As you review your current goals and objectives or write new ones,
you should compare them against your values, vision, and mission, and
new guiding principles to determine if they are consistent with these. Do
they abide or stay within the guidelines that your principles dictate? Are
they in violation of your values? Do they further your vision and mission?
These are very important issues to discuss. Without these conversations,
your metaphor will never be given the "permission" to transform your
organization. In other words, in drifting away from the process of comparing, you will not be giving full access to the metaphor to influence
your goals and objectives. In time, you will find yourself reverting back

to your old ways and conclude, incorrectly, that metaforming is not a valuable tool for transformation.

Metaforming must be applied systematically as you review your goals and objectives. The temptation will be to skip over or let things remain as they are. You will have wasted valuable time and money if this is the case. Applying the new metaphor requires that everyone in the organization be fully vested in the process. From the board of directors to the entry level positions, everyone should know what you are trying to achieve. They should fully understand the metaphor and the process. The CEO needs to be the driver for the change. He or she will have to devote considerable time to the change since transformation is an all-encompassing exercise. As various people in the organization catch on, delegation can take place, however, the CEO must remain actively involved and supportive of the transformation.

Know the Condition of Your Employees

Many people in the organization may feel unsettled or complacent about the proposed changes. This could be from any number of issues such as fear of the unknown, fear of loss, fear of failure, disruption of relationships, personality conflicts, politics, or cultural assumptions and values. It is important in your communication to empathize with these feelings regardless if you agree with them or not.

At some point early on, you will need to create a sense of urgency. You will need to shake up the equilibrium so that some form of change will be expected. The organization would not be facing the need for transformation unless they had not already recognized signals that were disconcerting either in the marketplace, with their customers or clients, or with the direction of the industry in general.

Next, it is important to pull together a coalition of supportive leaders who can guide the organization through the transformation process. These leaders may not all hold positional authority. Some may have influence due to their expertise, their personality, or their length of time at the company. Regardless, you will need to gather the key influencers and work together with them to move the organization forward.

As you begin the change process you will need to eliminate any rewards for current behavior that will be undesirable in the transformed organization. This could involve discouraging water cooler talk or long lunch breaks. In times past, you may even have participated in behaviors that would not be tolerated in the new organization. You will need to assess situations as they come up to determine if by participating, you would be encouraging these behaviors.

All along the change continuum, you will need to move the organization to initiate new options and explain their rationale. This can be accomplished in a rewards system where you celebrate desired behaviors by implementing new rituals. Some organizations celebrate new sales, promotions, cost-cutting measures, and serving one another. At some point, as you near completion of the change process you can formalize the reward system through policies and procedures that ensure standardized processes and equal opportunity is afforded to participate and be rewarded.

Using Change Agents

Many organizations use internal staff to serve as change agents through the process. They act as monitors and trackers of the change. When they see things that are not getting completed or behind schedule, they report to those in authority to get the organization back on track. Sometimes they have been delegated the authority by the CEO to take action when necessary. Some of the advantages to using internal staff are that they know the history, the political system, and the culture of the organization. In addition, they will have to live with the results so they are vested in the transformation. Some disadvantages are that they may be associated with certain groups or factions and be accused of favoritism. They may also be too close to the issues to provide an objective perspective.

Some organizations use external consultants to serve as change agents. The advantage of this is that they can bring an objective and impartial perspective. The disadvantage is that they have limited knowledge of the organization, its politics, and the culture; however, this can be overcome with a thorough fact-finding process. They may also be viewed with suspicion. Whichever approach your organization takes, the change agents must be trusted and seen as experts with proven track records to their counterparts in the organization.

Training Is Essential

Transformation of an organization often requires training in new skills such as leadership, executive coaching, job redesign, conflict management, emotional intelligence, or high-performance team building. The worst thing an organization can do is to require their employees to engage in new behaviors or skills and not prepare them properly. Unfortunately, many organizations leave out the preparation due to costs or the time involved to facilitate this part of the transformation process. This is a fatal mistake and can literally derail the entire process. Incredible metaphors cannot help an organization that wants to short cut things in order to try to save a few dollars. Transformation is an all-or-nothing proposition. The organization's health and existence may depend on it. As you can see metaplying is an involved process; but if done correctly and with commitment, your organization can find fresh wind to propel it into a new ocean.

Learning Reinforcement Exercise

1. Your guiding coalition is your leadership team who are supportive of the transformation initiative.
   Circle: True   False

2. Internal change agents know the history, politics, and culture of the organization but may be held in suspicion because of alignment with certain factions or groups.
   Circle: True   False

3. External consultants serving as change agents can provide an objective perspective and must be seen as experts in their fields but not equivalent to their counterparts in the organization.
   Circle: True   False

Answers are Italicized:

1. Your guiding coalition is your leadership team who are supportive of the transformation initiative.
   Circle: *True*   False

2. Internal change agents know the history, politics, and culture of the organization but may be held in suspicion because of alignment with certain factions or groups.

   Circle: *True*   False

3. External consultants serving as change agents can provide an objective perspective and must be seen as experts in their fields but not equivalent to their counterparts in the organization.

   Circle: *True*   False

PART 5

Serving Up a New Metaphor

CHAPTER 13

The Work of the Metaphor

The serve was invented so that the net could play.
—Bill Cosby

The Executive Team meetings continued through the autumn months and into Christmas. They put things on hold until after the New Year celebration but jumped back on it in January. By late spring, they were well on their way to a complete overhaul of the company from the vision statement right down through every aspect of the organization. They had to ask some pretty tough questions along the way. They got some people pretty shook up. Jason tried to keep everyone focused on the new vision of the company by talking regularly about the tennis ball metaphor. He even brought a tennis ball to every staff meeting and when someone wanted to speak, whoever had the ball in his or her possession at the time would toss it to the person speaking. This kept the metaphor before them. Jason started carrying the tennis ball with him most of the time he was at work.

They began the process by going back to their chart that described the attributes of the tennis ball and breaking down the organizational principles one by one. Two principles stood out as being similar: the ability to be flexible and resilient.

Their organization had gotten so large and cumbersome that by the time they recognized they were losing market share to their competition, it was almost too late. They were unable to respond to changing conditions quickly. Attacks on their customer base were crippling and difficult to recover from. This pointed to the need to slim down the organization. Intuitively, Jason knew this all along but didn't want to face the fact that they had a lot of excess weight. They added a column to their chart of attributes and principles to list some actions they could take to respond to the principles. Whenever possible, Jason required these to be listed as action verbs. He wanted their tasks to be proactive and not reactive. He wanted to build momentum in the organization and get everyone looking at every activity and how, or if it furthered our organization in the spirit of the metaphor.

New attributes	Guiding principles	Actions
Energetic	Do things that inject energy into the daily life of the organization.	Celebrate victories weekly. Address every challenge as an opportunity.
Focused	Stay focused on the vision.	Make sure everyone can recite the vision, and require everyone to provide at least three examples during the quarter when they had done things that supported the vision.
Right size	Be willing to become the size of organization that you want, not what others say you should become.	Downsize and reorganize around core competencies. Be agile.
Motivated	Find ways to keep everyone motivated at all times.	Take opportunities to thank good performers daily. Do something special for them weekly.
Full of Joy	Make sure to maintain a joyful workplace culture.	Weave rituals and artifacts into the culture of the organization. Celebrate birthdays and let people know they are valued on a daily basis.
Flexible	Design an organizational structure that can flex with the times and situations.	Flatten the organization.
Decisive	Make sure the decision-making process is not cumbersome.	Remove unnecessary decision points. Allow people to make decisions at their level.
Free	Be willing to take risks.	Entertain even the most ridiculous sounding initiatives. Don't wait until everything is perfect to launch a new artist or project.
Resilient	Don't take life too seriously and always look to the good in every outcome.	Laugh often. Discuss outcomes openly and what we could learn from them.

Planning Our Assessment

They began planning the assessment of their situation by taking the 30,000-foot look and drilling down. They chose to view the company through three lenses, the organizational design lens, the political lens, and the cultural lens. Each of these would give them a pretty good idea where they needed to concentrate their energies and what were some of the potential challenges they would face in the coming months.

The organizational design lens allowed them to see how the flow of certain tasks and information was designed and how their employees were sorted into various roles. They also saw how these roles were related to each other, and the optimal design they needed to remain consistent with the new metaphor and the principles that they derived from the attributes. There were three elements they examined that helped them manage the amount of information they were gathering; grouping, linking, and alignment.

They first considered grouping, or how things differentiated themselves from other things. They drew boundaries around clusters of tasks or activities. This helped them to define jobs, departments, and associated processes. The task is the core element of the design of an organization. It is the smallest unit of activity that must be performed to realize organizational goals. Tasks vary in complexity, how often they are performed, and if they are interdependent with other tasks. Sometimes certain tasks must be completed before another related task can begin. Sometimes related tasks can be completed concurrently while others are completed in a repetitive manner by interacting with each other.

As they looked at how their people were grouped, they realized that this varied by expertise or function, by output or product, or by the market, either geographically or by customer group. Jason could see this was going to take time to analyze the organization.

Next they looked at how departments and roles were linked across these boundaries. This provided them an understanding as to how things were integrated within the organization. One primary linking mechanism they looked at was the formal reporting structure, the organizational chart. This showed them the hierarchical design of the company. They looked at which roles were liaison type roles. These people interacted across departments and work team boundaries. They looked at integrator roles, people who were able to bring various concepts and processes into the overall picture. They also took a deep look at their information technology systems to determine if, in the new metaphor, they would need something different or whether their current IT configuration would be adequate. Finally, they looked at how they handled planning, who was involved, how things were tasked, and how they maintained accountability. They were definitely deficient in their ability to maintain accountability.

The team recognized that alignment of the organization would ensure that everyone has the necessary resources and is motivated to complete the work they've been assigned. This involved looking at various systems. They found some of this information in their employee's handbook, but much of it was outdated or not followed as part of their daily activities. They first looked at their employee performance measurement systems. They had one but they didn't use it well. Everyone seemed to be rated at the top of the scale, if and when they were evaluated. They considered their rewards and incentives program. This had dropped to the wayside a long time ago. Jason suspected this contributed to some of the grumbling that a couple of his supervisors were dealing with. They looked at their budgeting process and how they allocated funds. They also went through their entire Human Resources Development plan. It was pretty weak. It seemed that after they hired and provided initial training for someone, they did very little to get them ready for promotions. There were few identifiable career paths in the various departments.

They knew that redesigning the organization would not be without its problems. They would have to disrupt the normal flow of business. A redesign could create problems with long-term relationships they had with some key customers and suppliers. It would certainly create stress and anxiety with all their employees; however, they knew they had to do this.

Next, they looked at the organization through the political lens. At first, two of Jason's Executive Team members pushed back on this. They struggled to acknowledge that they had a culture that included office politics. Jason thought they wanted to turn a blind eye to this. In actuality, they were two of the biggest politically savvy leaders in the organization and took advantage of this every opportunity they could.

Some of the core concepts of the political lens they had to consider included interests and power. The entire organization is grounded in the various interests that are held by members and groups in the company. They certainly had cliques and they usually wanted things their way. All the stakeholders from the Board members, through the Executive Team, and all the way down to the mailroom and warehouse folks had special interests. These could be personal or business related. They had to analyze what interests were represented and the priorities they held individually and from the corporate point of view.

Politics is about the ability to influence others. It includes personal characteristics, scarce and valued expertise, past performance and track records, the formal position in the company, and informal relationships or social networks. They discovered that the influence from social networks was often stronger than from positional authority. They knew in order to bring about the changes they needed, they would have to develop successful political strategies. They needed to determine where interests were and the power that these interest groups held. They had to get "buy-in" throughout the organization or they stood to lose some very important colleagues. They had to find allies and build a coalition as well as networks. All of this would require them to sharpen their negotiation skills.

As they looked at networks, they realized that there were three basic types: advice networks, trust networks, and communication networks. Advice networks centered on those people who could solve problems. These folks were usually pretty highly trained and with considerable experience. Most of their technical people and art department types fit here. The trust network was kind of like an informal "grapevine" where gossip was passed up and down the organization. Over the years Jason had benefitted from asking his admin assistant what was going on. She was well tied into the grapevine. The grapevine was part of the communication network, which involved the various work-related conversations that took place each day. Some were formal and some informal.

The last lens they looked at was the cultural lens that focuses on the meanings that people give to what they experience at work. The symbols or artifacts that represent things throughout the organization tell a lot about the culture. The team knew that in the early days of the business, their culture was pretty laid back. They dressed casually, no one used titles, and they all played together outside of work. However, over the years, they had become more formal in how they engaged each other. Groups of people stayed to themselves. About the only time they got together in a large setting was at the annual company picnic that they traditionally held at Doheny State Beach Park. Jason remembered some great times there. The company purchased all the meat, usually tritip and chicken. Everyone else brought salads, rolls, vegetables, and desserts. They grilled all day, played beach volleyball and flag football, and paddled kayaks. They held the picnics during the last Friday in June because Jason always thought that it meant more if everyone had a workday off to celebrate together rather than ask someone to use their Saturday for a company picnic.

They also looked at the subcultures within the organization. This was usually segregated by the genre of music that the individuals were involved with. They would often take on the dress and the posture of the artists. You could easily identify the hip-hoppers from the pop folks. The rockers were a breed unto themselves.

Implementing the Assessment

After organizing their assessment process around the three lenses of strategic design, political, and cultural aspects, one of the very first actions they initiated was an audit of all their job descriptions, communication channels, and organizational structure. By combining the results of these with a process inventory, they were able to identify several significant redundancies, which when eliminated, reduced their costs and increased their efficiencies.

Through interviews, they also identified a number of people who were in positions where they were either not well qualified or were unhappy in their roles. They found several people were overcompensated and several were undercompensated. They had not been systematic in handling their compensation packages, and that had created some hard feelings among some of the staff.

During this time, everyone was feeling a lot of uncertainty. They were concerned not only about their jobs, but also about how the changes would affect the environment at the office. Almost everyone had regular routines that they tried to maintain. Some would stop at Starbucks or their favorite caffeine injection joint on the way to work. They would often meet friends there and hang out for a while. Because of the nature of their work, keeping regular office hours was not always possible. This created a lack of accountability that was enjoyed by many. In some ways, there were members of the staff who saw this as a part-time job. They had other things going on in their lives and their work became second to everything. There really was no way to allay anyone's fears that things were going to change. Unfortunately, no one knew quite how great the changes would be.

As they progressed into the early stages of change, many were reluctant to address change adequately in their behavior, timelines, and their willingness to work toward the change. Some tried to do business as usual, just slowly moving along, late for meetings, not prepared, waiting for others to do the work, and contributing very little to the success of the company.

Many had joined the organization in the last few years. Although it was still somewhat nimble before they arrived, it had put on weight, and the pace had slowed quite a bit. Trying to talk to the newer employees about a company that existed before they were hired was difficult for them to comprehend. It was only the old timers such as Jason who understood what they had been and what they could become. He knew that he needed to create a sense of urgency in order to motivate others with the need to change.

Time for a Town Hall Meeting

Jason called a town hall meeting to discuss the situation with everyone. Prior to the meeting, he met with some key Executive Team members, those with the greatest influence. He also met with key supervisors and a few experienced people who were respected by the rest of the employees. During these meetings he let them in on all they had become. Some, particularly those who were not on the Executive Team, were not aware of their numbers and how the company had started to take a very long slide into possible oblivion. He asked for their support and told them that after the town hall meeting, he wanted to meet again to map out a communication plan so that they could get as many of their staff on board as possible.

Unbeknownst to them, he had put together a chart that listed the names of Executive Team members and key leaders throughout the organization.

This chart categorized each of them as to where Jason thought they were on a change continuum line from, "dig in their heels" on the far left, to "early adopters" on the far right. He could see that they had a lot of work to do to get some of them to change their way of thinking. In the end, they would either get onboard or they would not be able to stay with the organization. He knew, however, that he needed to build a coalition of leaders to help guide the organization through the difficult days ahead.

The film and television executives were well liked and carried considerable influence throughout the organization. Jason knew they would have some issues to discuss that directly involved their departments, and he was concerned whether they would be supportive of the change that needed to take place. Their departments were the glamorous ones. Everyday they had television and movie stars in their offices, and many young employees wanted to work there to rub shoulders with the celebrities. They were star struck, but that was expected until they got used to seeing how human the celebrities were, sometimes too human! Jason figured he would need to meet alone with the executives of these two units in the near future.

In the town hall meeting, Jason talked about the history of the company. He shared old pictures of some of them who were there in the beginning. Several of them stood with him in front in the large multipurpose room where they met for all-hands gatherings. There were some nervous laughs as they flipped through the pictures. He told them about their first Billboard #1 artist and how they felt when they got the good news. He thought some of them struggled to relate to that feeling since many of their artists had hit that threshold many times during their career. He also talked about how they started as a small family and had grown into a company that included every ethnicity, race, gender, and generation. They were as diverse as any organization out there and got along reasonably well. Then, he had to talk about where they were and what they had become.

Jason mentioned their strengths and their weaknesses. Their weaknesses seemed to outweigh their strengths, however. He talked about some of the painful possibilities, most of which were likely unless they changed course. He also talked about a timeline. It was then that it became very real for most of them. The room got really quiet. He broke the silence by telling them that the worst did not have to happen if everyone got serious about changing from what the organization had become to where they needed to go. It would not be easy but it was possible. He ended the meeting with everyone joining hands, and while they were represented by every faith and worldview, he prayed long and hard. It was a somber and sobering moment.

The day following the town hall meeting Jason met with the key leaders again to talk about how to communicate with the employees so that they could remain informed. He knew that rumors would be flying around like bees around a hive. He didn't want people to start taking their frustrations out on each other, so keeping clear communication channels open was critical. He had the IT folks set up a private, in house, website that was accessible only by the employees. He thought about including their suppliers and distributors since they had such a close relationship, but he decided against it for the moment. He did meet with CEOs from each supplier and distributor early in the process to explain what they were doing and how they were going to do it. They seemed satisfied that his company wasn't pulling out of the marketplace. This new website included updates, calls to meetings, and a place where people could blog about various change-related issues. He let everyone know that no one would be penalized or disciplined for posting honest thoughts and feelings. He tried to monitor it every day so that he could keep his finger on the pulse of the rumor mill. There were a couple of yelling incidents in the parking lot between disgruntled employees during the next few months but nothing serious.

The leadership had to make some very tough decisions in the days to come by letting some people go. Jason was pretty well connected in the industry and was able to help most of them find positions with other companies: some with suppliers, some with distributors, and some with their competition. Their competitors were pretty surprised and a bit suspicious of their motives. However, after they did their due diligence, they knew that Jason's organization was just trying to do the best thing for their employees. Several of their competitors even called and thanked him personally for sending them some excellent people.

The employees that they had let go were also pretty surprised that Jason went out of his way to help them get hired within the industry. He thought it did a lot for their reputation, but most of all it was the right thing to do. Many of these people had been with the organization for several years and had become a part of their family. Unfortunately, the family had gotten too large. After getting their organizational structure in order, they went about reassessing their vision and mission statements.

Reworking Vision and Mission Statements

Organizational work on the vision statement took a considerable amount of time. The leadership wanted to get things just right. Their old vision statement evolved from, "To be an international force in music that would change the lives of everyone who heard or saw the incredible mix of sound or visual performance by their artists and productions," to "To live music." This was short, concise, and projected the action of living rather than merely "being." A tennis ball is at its best when it is moving through the air, traveling to a destination. Their company was operating at its best only so long as they were being active, promoting, producing, and delivering good music content.

Next, they looked at their mission statement. They started with, "Their mission is to make international stars of their artists by producing and promoting their work around the world to audiences of every class, race, and ethnic group," to "Their mission is to activate a global response by serving the best music possible to their audience." This new mission statement included two action words, "activate" and "serving." Both of these represented the trajectory of a tennis ball sailing through space. They wanted to show speed and action while being careful not to define any particular response by their audience to the music that they presented.

While their clients included the musicians themselves, in the old mission statement they had elevated them above their audience. Instead, they wanted their mission to reach beyond their musicians to their audience and therefore took the focus off the musicians and on the content of entertainment value to the customer.

Aligning to Values, Culture, and Leadership Performance

One thing organization leaders had struggled with for many years was the ability to align their actions to their values. They had no way to measure their soft people skills such as corporate cultural fit and leadership performance and therefore alignment existed only on paper. During this time of reevaluation, Jason came across a product by a company that had developed a tool that measured soft people skills and plotted these as well as performance on a Cartesian grid. The tool allowed them to plan, track, and assess everyone's performance.

They implemented training to help those deficient in certain behaviors or performance. This tool, along with the training, helped them ensure their success in the future.

Questions to Consider

1. Using the guiding principles you considered at the end of Chapter 9, identify some actions that your organization might take that would line up with these guiding principles.
2. What are some steps that you would take to assess your organization's effectiveness?
3. How would you communicate the results of this assessment within the organization?
4. Using the new metaphor that you created in Chapter 10, how might your new vision and mission statements differ from your old ones?

CHAPTER 14

The Impact of the New Metaphor

You shake my nerves and you rattle my brains
—Jerry Lee Lewis, "Great Balls of Fire"

At this point the team had to roll the metaphor down into their goals and further into their objectives. The department heads were very involved in this process because these were strategic and tactical choices that needed to be made. What and how these were written, who was given responsibility, what resources were made available, and what timeframes and deadlines were established affected everyone. By this time, Jason thought most people were getting the hang of this. They were beginning to appreciate the metaphor and what it could do for their company.

The metaphor affected those outside the company as well as internally. Jason talked to management about some of the challenges they faced. The company did most of the music production and packaging activities in-house. In the early days, they subcontracted a lot of this, but because they wanted greater control they brought this in house, which came with a price tag. They had rising labor costs due to benefits increases and some unionization. The people were certainly worth the money, but their budget had ballooned and they were pricing themselves out of the market. As a result of discussions, the company went back to subcontracting some services. This allowed smaller vendors to get in the game and also supported a competitive pricing model that was healthy for their industry in general. At first quality was a concern, but the subcontractors really stepped up and provided some excellent work.

One thing that Jason had been dreading was the idea of having to look at their artist roster and consider letting some go. The career of an artist has its ups and downs, and musicians are in one of the most challenging and potentially heart-breaking professions. There are no less than a dozen or more people involved in keeping an artist's career alive and on the front burner with audiences. Management knew they had to cut their roster.

Changes Create Opportunities

Jason had several old friends on that roster. They had grown up in the business together. He personally went to each of them and broke the news. It was not easy. However, while he was driving to the mansion home of his first musician friend, he came upon an idea. The music industry is full of young, aspiring musicians new to Los Angeles and new to the industry. Jason decided to spin off another company that would train, mentor, and coach young artists. What he really needed was seasoned musicians who would be willing to give back some of their experience to help these young, inexperienced artists.

When Jason pitched this idea to his first old friend, she was indignant. She was a pop idol. She was a star for goodness sake, albeit an aging one. How could she ever have the time to baby-sit young musicians? However, after she considered more deeply what Jason was proposing, she began to warm up to the idea. He had his first mentor/coach, and they launched the musician's mentoring program. He was able to sign on seven of 10 seasoned musicians that the company was letting go. They didn't do it for the money though. Jason reminded each of them what it was like when they first started out. They talked about old times, sitting around eating at places like the Rainbow Bar and Grill and Dukes Coffee Shop, while talking about who got this gig, who was putting out some gnarly tunes, what new albums or singles were charting. They spent many hours commiserating together. They bonded. But now it was a different season for the musicians as it was for Jason's label. They could really leave a great legacy if they were willing to help these young musicians. It hit a chord with them, and they got very enthusiastic. Several of them were also willing to help bankroll the idea.

Along with letting some of their older musicians go, the company had to get aggressive in finding new talent. This required them to go on the hunt. When they found musicians with potential, they spent a lot of time grooming them, preparing them for stardom. They hit it sometimes but more often they missed, as is the nature of the music business.

Along with finding new talent, the company had to get more aggressive finding good songs. These go hand in hand. For a long time, they had developed their in-house writing staff. However, their success had waned over the past few years. They decided to let many of these writers go and instead work the streets for new compositions. They needed to add to their catalog. There were a lot of young songwriters who were hungry to get their work recorded and published, and once the news got out that Jason and his team were looking, they were flooded with some incredible songs. Some were very innovative, the type that the company would have shied away from in the past. But they knew for them to get competitive again, they would have to take chances and risk having a flop now and then.

Major Cuts in Every Corner

The company's television and film business had required a huge initial investment in time and money. They had broken even over the years, but things had started to slow as the major competitors got bigger and bigger. The conglomerates had taken over the television and film business, and Jason's organization was simply too small to make any impact. Their costs were rising, and they were finding it increasingly difficult to find good scripts and adequate distribution. Jason met with the VPs of these departments to talk about options. These VPs were able to secure some funding and purchased the hard assets from Jason. They took about a 150 of their full-time staff with them. That was almost half of their operation but accounted for about three quarters of the production costs. It was a good parting. Jason was happy for them and wished them well. Jason's team produced a lot of film and television scores for them after that and worked to help them get their new film and television company launched.

Jason also had to trim his top executive staff. It was a sad day when he had to break the news to those who were his close friends. They had spent many hours together at his Malibu beach home, sitting and watching the vast ocean spread out before them, sipping on a glass of "cab" realizing how fortunate they were to be doing something they loved and getting paid to do it. A couple of the guys had Porsches too, and several times a year, they would take their wives on road trips up the winding Pacific Coast Highway to Carmel and other destinations. He wondered if their friendships would remain intact.

As they pared down their staff and Executive Team, they had to find ways to become more productive. There were so many things that they had to double up on, and their time had become their greatest commodity. In an effort to become more productive, they engaged a productivity consultant who was an amazing expert. Each day he sat with one of the members of the Executive Team and just watched how they handled their time. He would take notes, and at the end of the day he would tell each of them how to get more out of the hours they were spending at work. He also presented a workshop where he talked to staff about other ways they could become more productive and balanced in life. They found ways to give back more time to their families, come to work rested, and prepare for meetings and activities well in advance. Jason found himself functioning better than he had in years and not feeling like he was doing any more work than usual. However, Jason realized he was being more productive when he looked at the log he kept, which reflected how he was using his time. He was doing the work of two men, half his age. On top of that, he was getting in shape, sleeping better, and his mind was as sharp as a razor.

Through the years the company had hired a number of MBAs from top business schools. For the most part, they were good analysts but most lacked entrepreneurial fire. They could manage teams to accomplish objectives, but they didn't have the instincts to see new possibilities in a given situation. They were so focused on structured tasks that it was difficult for some of them to bounce off a wall they encountered and find a new trajectory. This was not a problem under their old metaphor; but as part of the new direction, there was little room for employees who were not entrepreneurs or intrapreneurs. They needed people who could think outside the box, who could serve up new approaches, and power slam innovative concepts past the competition. Jason let the department heads and Human Resources handle the layoffs but once again made every attempt to help them find new employment. Many were successful, and future encounters with them were pleasant.

As the organization downsized, they found themselves wandering around empty warehouses and offices. Some areas started to resemble a ghost town. Jason had mixed emotions. He knew they had to stay true to the new metaphor, but he was hurting inside like a person might if he didn't have enough food to feed the family. The company had to get leaner, faster, and more agile and resilient. They had gone on a diet and were now having to get in shape for the marathon. The empty spaces made them realize that the associated utility costs would kill them if they didn't make some adjustments. They developed a plan to sell off or rent out some of the space to their subcontractors. This put them in closer proximity and gave the subs much needed space to expand at a price that was slightly lower than the market. Everyone was happy.

The company had a large garage full of production trucks, company cars, and other vehicles. One by one, they sold off the rolling stock until they had only what they needed. Some of it was old but it was all in good shape, something that Jason had demanded. Because they had taken good care of everything, they were able to sell the trucks and cars at premium prices in an economy that was not very sympathetic to their restructuring efforts.

Questions to Consider

1. What opportunities could your new metaphor create for your organization?
2. What threats could your new metaphor create for your organization?
3. In what ways might the employees of your organization respond to the application of your new metaphor?
4. How might your new metaphor impact your future business?

CHAPTER 15

New Markets, New Employees, New Opportunities

She was more like a beauty queen from a movie scene
—Michael Jackson, "Billy Jean"

Throughout the restructuring and realigning, company leaders were constantly going over their marketing efforts. Even their branding had aged and the cracks were starting to show. They brought in a top branding consultant to help them match their branding to their new metaphor.

As part of the process, they took Jason's team through a series of workshops in which they stepped back and looked at their metaphor and the imaging that it represented. The consultant also had them write down their perceptions of their brand while coming up with a list of adjectives to describe it. Then they got together in small groups and shared their thoughts to see if they could find consistency. They were also required to identify their main brand attributes and check for consistency with their proposed marketing plan. It was a rigorous couple of days but it was well worth it. They ended up creating a series of ball-type images on trajectories reflecting speed and agility as the core of their new brand. The new branding campaign helped them win a "Brand Genius Award."[1]

The staff aggressively designed a new marketing campaign based upon their rebranding efforts. They started devoting more effort toward online marketing, network marketing, and guerilla-marketing techniques. These were things that were secondary strategies for them in the past. However, they had rested on their products and reputation until they could no longer sustain their previous momentum.

The company began actively injecting their new message into the new marketing strategies. They had to pay more attention to consumer behavior and their changing demands. They had to reach out to fans and connect to them through social media platforms. They had to start giving product away to build brand loyalty. They had to lower the price of their CDs in order to make them competitive with digital downloads. There were still many people who wanted a CD version for their library, but the company couldn't rely on this single market demand. They had to consider cutting deals with artists that involved revenue sharing. They had to develop new licensing agreements. They were willing to try anything at this point.

They had never been niche players in the past. That was usually the domain of the small independent labels. However, if they were going to make any effort to spin off a specialized genre department, the company needed to make sure the market was large enough to support their efforts. With the choice of smooth jazz as their genre, they knew that the target consumer was typically over 40, middle to upper middle class, and with significant disposable income. This opened up a new market for them, which would increase revenues over time. However, reaching this market would require them to adopt a modified marketing strategy.

Jason tasked the VP of Marketing to get started and not be afraid to take some risks. He reminded the VP that their new metaphor should embolden them to be risk takers. He helped the marketing department develop a relationship with a top smooth jazz station in Los Angeles. They also developed a strategic partnership with a posh hotel in Newport Beach and the radio station to sponsor jazz concerts as part of their Jazz Concert Series. They were increasing their visibility in this market very quickly.

Adding New Blood

Although they had been letting many people go, they also started hiring some younger marketing geniuses to work for them full time. Their appearance and attire caused the company's leadership to blink at the somewhat circus-like atmosphere that was being created in their workspaces. They tore down a number of walls in order to open up the spaces into bullpen areas where they could see almost everyone, managers included. For some of the old timers, this was a bit uncomfortable. They were used to hiding out in their offices, managing their portfolios, and making lunch dates with buddies in the business. Now, they were forced to actively engage their teams.

As company personnel found their rhythm, they discovered they were starting to enjoy the new energy that the younger crew was bringing to daily activities. Some of the older guys got rid of their ties and started wearing jeans to work. This was quite a departure from recent times. But as Jason thought back on it, they all wore jeans when the company started out. He didn't remember when this all changed, but it was nice to get back to the days when they were more concerned about making and selling music than they were about managing their portfolios.

The buzz started to get around in the industry. Competitors were not sure what was happening, but they were seeing things starting to change. Jason's team was on the streets and more visible than they had been for a long time. They were present in meetings and at showcases late at night.

For the most part, they had long since quit going to showcases where new talent would present their acts or songwriters would introduce new songs. It used to be that Jason spent at least four nights a week attending one showcase or another. It became exciting again to see the new raw talent laying everything on the line to get a record deal.

The company's approach in the last few years had been to buy out contracts of artists that had broken into the marketplace under smaller independent labels. In this way, these smaller labels took all the risks, and Jason and his team were able to pick up promising artists on their way to the top without all the developmental costs. However, this had to change as well. They started taking risks with new artists. While this was unheard of by companies their size, it paid off over time.

Improving the Manufacturing Processes

In the area of product, they had been batch shipping for a number of years. This allowed them to maintain some control of production costs but it also required them to warehouse music products. Warehousing costs are not cheap, and because they had been selling off and renting their warehouse space, they no longer had the ability to maintain large inventories. In order to be consistent with the guiding principle of being agile, they moved to a lean engineering model and manufactured and shipped within a day of receiving orders. They found that they could also save some labor costs since they didn't have excess labor capacity working the warehouse.

Moving to a lean manufacturing process required them to work more closely with suppliers. Since they didn't have room to store production and shipping materials, their suppliers would have to respond to their orders more quickly than they had in the past. They also approached some of their suppliers and worked deals so that the supplier could rent the warehouse and one office space renter purchase the building at a discount. Jason's company personnel could literally walk next door and ask for supplies to be forklifted to their packaging facility, which was only 30 yards away.

Putting Fun Back in the Workplace

From a leadership perspective, monitoring the changing culture was very critical. In the early days, the work had been fun and exciting. Company personnel would ring a big bell in the reception lobby each time an artist hit the top 100. When they hit the top 10, they had a siren that Jason controlled and he would blast it, take out the cheap champagne, and pass around the bottle. It was truly a blast. As he thought back, they hadn't done that kind of thing for quite some time. He was not even sure when the practice stopped, but they rarely celebrated anything anymore.

Jason knew that they needed to come up with some new rituals and artifacts that would help them reengineer their culture. Rituals such as celebrating birthdays bring a group of people together, and the act of celebrating things that they all had a hand in doing created a camaraderie that would propel them into the next activity. He started to think about thresholds they could establish with varying degrees of celebratory activity. The first thing he did was to reinstitute the bell and the horn blast and gave control of it to the VP of Artists and Repertoire. Jason told him not to miss any occasion to make noise about the success of an artist.

On Fridays, everyone was to come to work in tennis attire. That didn't go over too well at first, but he allowed everyone to dress up their outfits to match their typical clothing styles. It was interesting to see one of the female employees dressed in a Goth-styled tennis outfit with chains and full Goth makeup. The company also had a fashion show during lunch with the winner receiving two complimentary tickets to the Comedy Store. The Goth employee won the first tickets. Everyone loved that. They threw in a bottle of cheap wine for pregame priming.

Naturally, the company went back to celebrating birthdays. On the third Wednesday of the month, they ordered a large cake for everyone born in that month. Employees had to attend the cake cutting and be prepared as a group to sing the song of the highest rated single from one of their artists that week. Believe it or not, everyone working in the music business is not musically inclined, and it was horribly apparent on several occasions. Jason made a mental note not to go out with them for a Karaoke night.

Teams were formed made up of employees from the various departments. They would often adopt team colors, chants, and tribal poles. A couple of times senior management had to step in to make sure things didn't get out of hand. The team with the highest charting artist in their category each week was able to proudly display a tribal pole made by the Art Department that was made from a tennis racket and tennis ball. They called it the Wimbledon Slam Award, and it was beautiful. Speed, quality, and innovation, which were consistent with their metaphor, became the metrics used to identify winning teams. Teams competed in a variety of ways, with winners receiving weekend passes to Disneyland, Knott's Berry Farm, or LEGOLAND.

Questions to Consider

1. As you consider your new metaphor, does it require rebranding efforts?
2. Do you see making changes with members of your current staff?
3. What can you do to improve your internal processes?
4. Can you identify new markets where your products or services might find opportunities?
5. What are some rituals and artifacts that would enhance the working environment for your employees?

PART 6

Structural Mapping

CHAPTER 16

The Structural Mapping Engine (SME) Process

I really love your peaches, wanna shake your tree.
—Steve Miller, "The Joker"

The structural mapping engine (SME) process[1] can help accomplish several things. Structural mapping is based upon the work of Dedre Gentner, most currently a professor in the Department of Psychology at Northwestern University. Gentner's structural mapping revolves around the idea that in an analogy or metaphor, one idea can be mapped onto another. This process was carried forward by Ken Forbus to develop the SME process. This process can identify appropriate pairs for your metaphor; point to operational principles, and from there, you can write your goals and outcomes so that they are consistent with the metaphor. Care should be taken when identifying appropriate pairs for your metaphor to assure that everyone is clear on the relationship between the target and the vehicle, and vice versa. SME uses a three-stage model local-to-global matching process to determine the maximum breadth of structural alignment between pairs of attributes. This offers the user the broadest number and gradient of pairings and their metaphorical relationships to draw on.

Stages of SME

The first stage involves the local matching stage. This is a symmetrical comparison activity in which attributes are defined and used to predict the potential matching pairs.[2] Let's look at the following metaphor. "The organization is a cruise liner" presents the target—the organization, and the vehicle—a cruise liner. Several attributes can be derived from the organization such as culture, politics, and strategy. An organization's culture dictates how personnel do things on a daily basis. It is characterized by how personnel respond to various external threats. Politics also impacts the speed with which an organization is able to make decisions. Bureaucratic, hierarchical organizations tend to move much more slowly than flatter organizations. Most organizations have some sort of strategy that guides them into their future. The attributes of cruise liners would be their inability to react or turn quickly. They are large and don't move fast. They have a set course, but they can veer off just by turning one degree from their intended track. The attributes of the organization and the cruise liner can be paired in the following ways, culture > reacts slowly, politics > moves slowly, or strategy > gets off track. They can be recombined until the all pairings are exhausted, culture > moves slowly, culture > gets off track, politics > reacts slowly, politics > gets off track, or strategy > reacts slowly, and strategy > moves slowly.

Stage 1

Original pairing
culture > reacts slowly
politics > moves slowly
strategy > gets off track
culture > moves slowly
culture > gets off track
politics > reacts slowly
politics > gets off track
strategy > reacts slowly
strategy > moves slowly

Stage two involves making sure structural consistency is enforced, which results in culture > reacts slowly, strategy > gets off track, politics > reacts slowly, and strategy > moves slowly as the most aligned structures.

Stage 2

Original pairing	Structurally consistent pairs
culture > reacts slowly	culture > reacts slowly
politics > moves slowly	politics > moves slowly
strategy > gets off track	strategy > gets off track

(Continued)

Stage 2 (Continued)

Original pairing	Structurally consistent pairs
culture > moves slowly	
culture > gets off track	
politics > reacts slowly	
politics > gets off track	
strategy > reacts slowly	
strategy > moves slowly	

In Stage three, inferences are established in the metaphor using structurally consistent pairings. What I mean by this is that the vehicle, a cruise liner, has attributes of reacting slowly, moving slowly, and getting off track. These attributes all point back to the target, which is the organization. They map or overlay themselves onto the organization and the associated attributes as shown in the previous chart. This mapping process conveys reacting slowly, moving slowly, and getting off track, to the target, which provides a more descriptive model to expand on. Taken in the broader sense, the organization reacts slowly when responding to its environment, often moves more slowly as it matures, and can get off track as it executes its strategy by growing into new markets, regions, and opportunities that were not intended as part of its strategic plan. Carrying this forward, the structurally consistent pairs point toward principles as demonstrated in the chart.

Stage 3

Original pairing	Structurally consistent pairs	Principles derived from consistent pairs of attributes
culture > reacts slowly	culture > reacts slowly	Organizations need to be sensitive to how their environments and changes to those environments may impact their culture and ultimately their ability to compete aggressively.
politics > moves slowly	politics > moves slowly	Organizations need to be sensitive to issues and the impact on their political environment and the time it takes to navigate the political climate and process.

(Continued)

Stage 3 (Continued)

Original pairing	Structurally consistent pairs	Principles derived from consistent pairs of attributes
culture > gets off track		
politics > reacts slowly		
politics > gets off track		
strategy > reacts slowly		
strategy > moves slowly		

From this example, I'm sure you can see any number of ways to apply these attributes to be prescriptive rather than just descriptive and thereby create goals and objectives. The organization needs to be sensitive to its environment and changes that may take place in order to remain competitive. To live and grow, the organization must be prepared to change its culture, navigate the political climate, and execute their strategy aggressively. These can be converted into goals and objectives written with action verbs as in the following chart.

Goals from Principles

Original pairing	Structurally consistent pairs	Principles derived from consistent pairs of attributes	Goals or objectives derived from principles
culture > reacts slowly	culture > reacts slowly	Organizations need to be sensitive to how their environments and changes to those environments may impact their culture and ultimately their ability to compete aggressively.	Meet weekly to discuss environmental changes and their potential impact on the organization's culture.
politics > moves slowly	politics > moves slowly	Organizations need to be sensitive to issues and the impact on their political environment and the time it takes to navigate the political climate and process.	Meet monthly to discuss issues and their impact on organizational politics. Discuss ways to prevent, as much as possible, the political process from slowing the organization's ability to operate successfully.

(Continued)

Goals from Principles (Continued)

Original pairing	Structurally consistent pairs	Principles derived from consistent pairs of attributes	Goals or objectives derived from principles
strategy > gets off track	strategy > gets off track	Organizations must be clear executing their strategies or they may find themselves in markets, regions, countries, or industries that they had not intended.	Conduct annual audits in order to maintain the organization's strategic direction. Consider any expansion decisions in light of the strategic plan.
culture > moves slowly			
culture > gets off track			
politics > reacts slowly			
politics > gets off track			
strategy > reacts slowly			
strategy > moves slowly			

While there are a number of complex methods that are beyond our discussion here, the preceding process should be sufficient to arrive at workable metaphors and translate them ultimately into actionable goals and objectives.

Symmetry and Direction

The previous metaphor points forward and works well as in, "The organization is a cruise liner." However, "A cruise liner is an organization," is less likely to be acceptable because the cruise liner is a ship. No mention is made of the crew, which make up an organization. If it stated, "The crew of a cruise liner is an organization," it would cease to be a metaphor but merely describing one type of organization. When the relationship points forward it is said to be directional. The attributes of the cruise liner, reacting slowly, moving slowly, and getting off course, point back to the organization and therefore, the relationship between the cruise liner and the organization is also asymmetrical. One domain is mapping its attributes onto the other, but not the other way around. The attributes of the cruise liner can be mapped onto the organization, but the attributes of the organization cannot be mapped onto the cruise liner.

Going back to the example of the record company, "The company is a tennis ball" works, but "the tennis ball is a company" does not. It is both directional and asymmetrical. This distinction is important when developing a metaphor. If the comparison is between two unlike yet equal things, the forward movement or propelling of one toward the other does not exist. This lack of movement potential does not serve the leader or the organization in so far as it does not increase, grow, or enhance either. Without this, the metaphor is merely descriptive and not prescriptive. Such a metaphor is only comparative in nature but not directional and asymmetrical. Without direction and asymmetry, it lacks transformative potential.

Organizational Transformation Potential

Transformative potential is important, particularly in the context of leadership and organizations. With regular change in the marketplace, leaders are constantly stretched to oversee more and more complex situations and environments. Organizations are continuously evolving, which requires them to change, adapt, test, grow, innovate, and conquer new markets. This constant stretching puts enormous pressure on the employees as they must also change, adapt, test, grow, innovate, and conquer their own biases, perspectives, and approaches to tasks and relationships.

The use of metaphors provides direction, propulsion, and motivation to help employees along, which allows the organization to evolve. This evolutionary process is one of growing without regard to size. An organization can grow by becoming smaller. This, however, is dependent on the metrics that the organization chooses to measure their evolutionary process. If it is revenue, then organizational capacity may be a predictor. If it is profit as a percentage of revenue, then a lean organization may have the advantage. This is up to the organization as they plot their course into the future. Regardless, however, leadership must affect this change through leading the organization on the right path, using effective strategies, and communicating these strategies in a manner that breathes life into the organization. Metaphors can be the vehicle to carry this message.

The greater the asymmetry of a metaphor, the greater is the transformative potential. However, this works only if structural alignment is maintained. "The organization is a cruise liner" works because it is structurally aligned. However, "The organization is a pencil" loses its structural alignment. "The organization is a fleet of cruise liners" works and creates added transformative potential by including numerous cruise liners in the metaphor. These could add more dimensions, which would permit more applications to the organization and its culture, politics, and strategy. Now let's go back and see how the record company is coming along.

Learning Reinforcement Exercise

1. Which of the following is not included in the three stages of the structural mapping engine (SME)?
   a. Local matching is derived
   b. Structural consistency is enforced
   c. Inferences are established
   d. Credibility is determined

Answer is italicized

1. The three stages of the Structural Mapping Engine (SME) are:
   a. *Local matching is derived*
   b. *Structural consistency is enforced*
   c. *Inferences are established*
   d. Credibility is determined

PART 7

Bouncing Back: 15–Love, and Back in the Game

CHAPTER 17

Upping the Stakes

I've been to the table, and I've lost it all before
I'm willin' and able, always comin' back for more
Squeezin' out a thin dime 'til there's no one hanging on my arm
I've gambled on a third time, a fool will tell you it's a charm
If I'm bettin' on a loser, I'm gonna have a devil to pay
But it's the only game I know to play, it doesn't matter anyway.
—Clint Black, "A Good Run of Bad Luck"

In a game of poker, the goal is to end up with a hand of cards that beats every other hand at the table. When bets are made, whether they are in the hundreds of dollars or merely matchsticks, each player must make the decision whether to play the round or fold. "Folding" means the player does not think he has a winning hand and opts out of the round while losing any money or matchsticks he has already bet. If the player opts to stay in, he must either "call" the hand or raise by increasing the pot. Calling the hand means he believes he has a winning hand and wants to end the game to determine if, in fact, he has won the hand. Sometimes, rather than merely "calling," a player will raise the stakes to increase the winning pot. The player may be confident of this move or may be merely bluffing in hopes that the other players will fold, thus allowing him or her to win the hand. At the record company, management was upping the stakes and not bluffing.

It had been three years since the company had adopted the new metaphor of the tennis ball, which served them well as they made organization-wide changes. The process, however, wasn't without its challenges. Jason realized that if he were to do it again, he would hire a consulting firm to help them through the process. Taking recommendations from consultants allows the organization's management to deflect controversy to some degree. Acting as an uninvolved third party allows the consultants to remain somewhat detached while having enough knowledge of the organization that they can be effective. Not all consulting firms understand the use and power of metaphors, so that would be something Jason would need to consider for the future.

Function Follows Structure

The new structure of the company's record label is probably the first and most visible result of the transformation. They flattened the organizational structure to give others more access to Jason and the other leaders. They were able to do this because they sold off the television and movie departments, and went from 15 vice presidents down to 7. They combined several of their remaining music departments and put directors and managers in charge with full authority to make decisions as long as they could justify how these decisions supported or activated elements of their vision and mission. Some of these were promotions, while others were demotions. Jason knew it was hard on those who were demoted. He tried to help them understand that the company needed to do this to align the organization with the vision and mission, which were aligned to the metaphor. They lost two highly gifted executives in the process.

A few promotions to managers opened up opportunities below them; however, the company didn't automatically fill these positions. Their assessment of job descriptions, the communication audit, and process audits revealed that they were overstaffed in some areas. As departments initially felt the pressure of trying to do all the work that had previously been done but now with less people, they discovered that some administrative activities were not needed.

The company also discovered that there were many processes that were redundant and replicated in other departments. They shut those processes down, though not unilaterally. They brought the affected departments together to work out the issues between them and presented an efficiency plan back to the now, much smaller, Executive Team.

Although the seven remaining members of the Executive Team reported directly to Jason, he also sought out regular input from the directors, managers, staff, and every person in the organization. At first, the senior leaders felt uncomfortable with this arrangement and pushed back.

They were concerned that their authority would be undermined. Jason realized that, as the CEO, he was the only one who could prevent this.

Jason brought the entire organization together for a town hall meeting, something that that had been started at the beginning of the transformation process. During one of the early town hall meetings, he told everyone about the new communication model, but he also told them that they should only use this open communication channel to him to provide feedback on processes, markets, customers, or their culture. It was never to be used to complain about someone up or down the chain. They would use other protocols through their Human Resources ombudsperson to address grievances of this sort. Jason was tested early on when a person in the warehouse tried to talk to him about her supervisor. Jason shut the person down pretty quickly, and it got around that he meant what he said. He never had this happen again.

The Right Tools and Training Make a Difference

The business management tool turned out to be a real godsend. In times past, the company was never able to measure soft people skills. The feedback in this area from performance reviews was always subjective in nature. Now, with a new method for quantifying soft skills, the management was able to identify poor cultural alignment with vision, mission, and values, as well as poor leadership skills. Another added benefit was that employees knew exactly what was expected of them, and how to achieve their performance and alignment goals. The guesswork had been taken out of the equation.

Jason could tell that the organization was becoming a fun place to work. People smiled more, were more ready to help one another, and took greater part in trying to solve problems that came along. They felt empowered because of the intensive leadership training they had received early on. First-year supervisors were required to attend regular leadership training courses, where they developed clear career paths to various leadership positions. With the business management tool, managers were able to identify those employees who were promotable one or two levels and made sure they were well prepared before they received their promotion opportunities.

With the success of the leadership training, the company decided to expand their training program. They had a consulting group bring in their catalog of courses in face-to-face and online formats. Their curriculum was extensive and was well received by employees. They set up an in-house skills university and taught courses year round. It went so well that some of their competitors found out and asked if they could send some of their staff to take courses. At first, the company thought this was odd, but they decided it would be a good way to build goodwill and a more collegial atmosphere in their industry. They charged a minimal fee and gained a lot of good PR in the process.

Questions to Consider

1. How would your new metaphor likely affect the organizational structure of your organization?
2. What tools could your employees and the organization benefit from as the change process is implemented?
3. What is your plan to provide these tools?

CHAPTER 18

Culture, Markets, and Personal Growth

Love is a Temple.
—From "One" U2

As part of their cultural enrichment initiative, the record company adopted a number of new rituals. The resulting employee satisfaction, expressed in follow-up surveys, convinced Jason that these rituals were critical to the overall health of the organization. Some were silly and some were profound. They helped the employees become stronger supporters of one another and, in many cases, close friends.

Leading the Market Again

The company had become a market leader in the genre of smooth jazz. Their artists were all charting, and they even had an artist as a regular radio commentator on the smooth jazz station. The Jazz Concert Series had become a huge hit in southern California. It was the place to go, with people buying season tickets well in advance. The exposure the company got was incredible, which added to the exposure of their artists. They even had one jazz artist invited to participate as an informal ambassador for the United States on a recent Department of Commerce junket to Beijing. The Chinese were really becoming avid smooth jazz fans. There is no language barrier when it comes to jazz. Their representation in the Pop and Hip-Hop circles was also still strong. They had artists charting, they were sponsoring concerts, and even promoting soft drinks as part of a licensing deal they had with a large beverage company. Their market share in all genres was up, and they had strengthened their distribution networks in developing countries because of some licensing and down-loading deals negotiated with strategic partners in these markets.

Jason was personally traveling a lot more. Before he could expect everyone to step up, he needed to step up first. It was important for the rest of the organization to see that he was leading from the front. That didn't mean that he was throwing his weight around, but he tried to lead by example. He figured they respected that. Jason was not afraid to jump in and get his hands dirty, but he didn't want to usurp roles and infringe upon anyone's creativity.

When the Executive Team started dressing down, everyone was a bit suspicious. Anyone above a supervisor usually dressed up for work. The rest of the organization wore jeans, so the uniform tended to get in the way by dividing the leadership from the rank and file. Jason didn't like that. He really enjoyed going back to his old tee shirts and jeans. He usually wore polo shirts so as not to seem too casual but he could throw on a sports jacket in the event that he had a meeting with some folks who were a bit more formal. You just never knew in this business. He had many good friends who wore jeans and casual shirts that were priced into the thousands of dollars for just one outfit. Jason had never fallen into that trap. He wore off-the-shelf Levi's and Costco Polo's. He wasn't out to try to impress anyone at his age, only to support the new metaphor.

Personal Transformation

Before the company started the transformation, Jason had been a bit over-weight, enough to resist tucking his shirts in. Other than an occasional stroll on the beach, he didn't get much exercise. When the organization got fat and lazy, he got fat and lazy. However, he didn't know which came first. When the organization became reenergized, Jason did as well. He had more energy now than when he was a young man in his early thirties.

Everyday brought with it an excitement that Jason had not experienced in a long time. He woke up looking forward to work and all that life had to throw at him that day. He anticipated how he would respond in various situations, and he was prepared. He still loved his Porsches, but now he was spending less time with them. Jason missed seeing some of his friends at the Porsche Club of America (PCA) breakfast meetings, but he was simply having so much fun at work that he didn't need the distraction.

His marriage was even transformed by the metaphor. He found that refocusing on the vision and mission of the business also caused him to do the same in his marriage. He became keenly aware of how his actions affected his wife and grown kids. He didn't bring a sour attitude home from the office. He was upbeat, full of energy, and thought of creative ways to love them. Jason and his wife spent more time together, and I don't mean just spending time together. They spent real, genuinely intimate time in each other's presence. He expressed an appreciation for her that he was not capable of doing in the past. She responded in the same way, and they found that their love had become so much stronger than before.

The Buzz

Apparently it had gotten around that Jason's label was the place to work. Their application pool had grown to the degree that they always had many more qualified applicants for a position than they needed and before they publicized it. The fact was though, that they seldom had to fill a position. They had implemented some great benefits in the way of a noncontributory retirement fund, daycare, increased personal and maternity leave for both genders, on-campus valet parking, flex time scheduling, and regular free financial counseling for every employee.

The company was getting applications from as far away as China, South Africa, and Australia. They had developed a strategic partnership with several universities in the area and were accepting interns on a regular basis. Unfortunately, because they had very few openings, they were unable to hire most after they graduated. They did, however, send them out to their competition with great letters of recommendation. They became the place to intern because of the excellent reputation they had developed in the industry. Everyone wanted to hire one of their young protégés.

Because they began spending more time on the streets identifying new talent, they had the pick of the litter, so to speak. They were at every showcase, not just in Los Angeles but also in Nashville, New York, and London. They had set up offices there specifically for this purpose. Their agents were like scouts for pro-football teams. They were continuously following up on leads and tracking down promising artists and writers.

If you saw one of their agents at a club or showcase, you were certain that someone there was being seriously considered for signing.

The representatives of the artists and writers loved working with the company and treated the relationship like a strategic alliance. They worked together to develop the artists, bring the right songs to the mix, and put together strong stage performances and career plans.

The spin-off artist mentoring company really took off as well. There was a waiting list to get into the program. Not only did the artists benefit, but the mentors were having the time of their lives. Some had even become close friends with their artists. One mentor passed away and left his estate, in excess of $42 million, to fund a retirement plan for all of their developing artists. It was simply amazing.

The company caught some flack early on from several competitors who couldn't understand why the organization was paring back in size. What the competition didn't understand at the time was that the company's focus had become laser sharp, and although they were paring back, they were gradually gaining market share. They quit trying to be everything to everybody. They did what they felt they could do best while treating their artists fairly and honorably. Some said they had lost their edge, but very quickly the naysayers discovered that was not the case. Jason's team became more competitive when it came to negotiations. They made concessions where they might not have in earlier years, but their concessions were not at the expense of reasonable profit.

Giving Back

As they were blessed financially, they gave more to charities around Los Angeles. They became big supporters of the Union Gospel Mission, and every Thanksgiving, their entire crew turned out to feed the homeless. They discovered that when they were serving others, they were finding a satisfaction and joy that they had never known. Their artists also began to catch on and offer to do concerts to raise money for this or that charity or good cause.

The company received a call from a well-known actor who had Parkinson's disease. Five of their top artists volunteered to perform at a fundraiser to find the cure. At a recent Grammy Awards, along with their artists sweeping the categories, their label was honored for their charitable giving. While they didn't do it for the acclaim, it was nice to see others begin to follow suit because of their willingness to bring up the needs of the poor and homeless to the rest of the music industry. Over the course of the last three years, they had been able to help raise in excess of $150 million, which was extremely rewarding.

Finally, company personnel had been transformed individually. They felt better about the work they were doing and who they were becoming individually and corporately. Jason tried to explain the concept of the power of the metaphor to a couple of old colleagues who didn't really get it. He told them if they wanted to know more they would have to wait for the book to come out. Here it is . . .

Questions to Consider

1. What are some areas in your personal life that you would like to change for the better?
2. What could you do to begin transforming these areas of your life? Manage your time better? Prioritize your personal relationships and activities? Schedule time for transforming activities?
3. How might the new metaphor help you in this transformation?
4. What are some ways that you and your organization give back to your local community?

CHAPTER 19

The Power of Words to Transform Through Metaphors

And I think it's gonna be a long long time
Till touch down brings me round again to find
I'm not the man they think I am at home
Oh no no no I'm a rocket man
Rocket man burning out his fuse up here alone.
—Elton John

As you've read through this book, you may have noticed that I've used metaphors to describe the various steps and processes in finding, deconstructing, interpreting, reconstructing, testing, and applying metaphors. Metaformation, as I call it, requires active engagement with language. Language can be a spectator's sport or a sport where one can get involved, get dirty, run fast, jump high, slam the ball, and leap over the net while dancing for victory. Language is a leader's primary tool, and as with any tool, learning how to use it properly will help you get the most use out of it.

I have always been fascinated with language. The greatest leaders of all time have wielded words with care when the situation was delicate, used them to slice into the hearts of followers to mobilize them for action, and slashed them about with great abandon in the heat of the battle to capture victory from the jaws of defeat. Metaphors have been used since before the time of Christ through the recent political campaigns. Great leaders have not always been the most educated. They were not necessarily the richest people. The language they used wasn't always their first language. But one thing is for certain; they knew how to use words to move the hearts of every person that heard them speak and saw them lead.

Organizations will always be with us in one form or another. They are the vehicles that bring people together to work for a common cause. Whether it is to make and sell a product, provide a needed service, or lead a nation to victory, leaders who understand the power of words and can string them together in metaphors of unequivocal strength will always have a role to play in history. History will showcase the legacy that they leave.

Their stories will melt into the fabric of humankind and become metaphors themselves. They will be the vehicles from which people will find strength, gain comfort, and build courage. "He is like Samson," they will say. "His wisdom is that of Solomon" will be their exclamation. "Her courage is like Anne Frank" will be the cry of the disenfranchised. Lest you not give yourself enough credit, remember, you too can be like Samson, with the wisdom of Solomon, and the courage of Anne Frank. It begins with your willingness to serve and then to lead. When you capture the heart of metaphors, it will beat in your veins and pulse in your forehead. Others will recognize that you have mastered the ability to use metaphors to bring transformation to their lives and organizations.

As you spend more time in metaphors, you will become adept at perceiving when to use them, choosing the most powerful in the given moment, and having the courage to speak change into existence. It will arrive on the tip of your tongue like a screaming fighter jet landing on an aircraft carrier. You will know it in the moment you say it, and others will perceive that you have something wonderful to say. You will be speaking life into their minds and then into their hearts.

The world has enough naysayers out there; those who want to be the first to cry out, "Unfair! They don't deserve it!" Don't be one of those. Be a leader who can see reality for what it is but is not willing to settle on it remaining that way. Be a leader who can rise above the voices of death and bring health and healing to others through encouraging words that are born out of the struggle of ideas in the midst of times that try men's souls. There is no rule, no statute, or no proclamation that requires you to bow to the lowly existence of mediocrity. You have the power to help others, and they will in turn help their organizations become beacons of light, piercing the darkness of financial crisis, and the struggle for life and prosperity. The power of words is an amazing thing, and you can master it through the use of metaphors. They will help you in the most difficult times as a leader. Sometimes you will use the metaphor of silence to overcome the opposition. Sometimes it will require the stringing together of several metaphors, each building on another until they burst forth with incredible insight into the problem. Metaphors can break down the walls of misunderstanding and bring clarity to the fight. Metaforming is not a difficult thing. It can become quite natural and flow easily from your lips. Practice it. It is an art as much as it is a science. You will learn to wax eloquent with words, structure, and meaning so that even you will be amazed at the impact you have on those who look to you for leadership.

Leaders like you who have just the right thing to say, at just the right moment, will bless your organizations. Your words will be like a gentle lotion that sooths hearts and minds. Follow the plan, follow the structure, but allow your creativity to flow over. Metaformation is the perfect opportunity to think with the left and right side of your brain simultaneously. You will merge creativity, inspiration, and analytics in the space of a few words. These words will slice through, cut out, and sew up as a surgeon's scalpel, and your audience will experience the healing they bring. Metaphors have that kind of power if wielded correctly. Use your new power for good and not for evil for you have been entrusted with a very important task, Leadership. Handle it with care. It is the most sacred of callings.

Endorsements

"A fascinating read with an autobiographical stance that draws the reader in and makes this book nearly impossible to put down! Dr. Jim Walz outlines an innovative, exciting, yet practical approach to goal achievement, which empowers both individuals and organizations alike to live out their values and vision to the fullest. Using his own life as an example and telling of how he has overcome significant challenges by harnessing and utilizing the power of words and imagery in order to achieve goals, Dr. Walz has ultimately created a go-to guide for reaching higher and higher levels of success in both business and life."

—Ivan Misner, PhD
NY Times Bestselling Author and Founder of BNI®

With over 6,000 chapters and 145,000 members worldwide, BNI is the largest business networking organization in the world. Last year alone, BNI generated 7.1 million referrals resulting in $3.3 billion worth of business for its members. We offer members the opportunity to share ideas, contacts and most importantly, business referrals.

"Dr. Jim Walz draws upon extensive experience in management along with a background in training and the entertainment community to share with management, at all levels, 'metaphors' for excellence in leadership. By pulling together familiar concepts in a new and interesting way, he has created the ultimate management handbook, which should be on every manager's bookshelf. His approach to 'meta4mation' will change the way we think about developing ourselves and our subordinates. Truly a handbook for present and future leaders alike."

—Dr. Paul Robere
Managing Director
Robere & Assocites (Thailand)
Member of the Deming Collaboration

"What an effective catalyst! Dr. Jim Walz has written a unique, creative and timely book that will both *inform* and *transform* our leadership effectiveness. Centering on the use of the metaphor as a tool of communication, it can build a bridge that significantly and positively impacts the target audience. What strikes me above all is his *purpose* in authoring this resource: that of helping all of us to become the best communicators possible— radically and richly producing positive change as individuals and leaders."

—Dr. Glenn C. Burris, Jr.

President

The Foursquare Church

The International Church of the Foursquare Gospel, commonly referred to as the Foursquare Church, is a Protestant denomination. As of 2000, it had a worldwide membership of over 8,000,000, with almost 60,000 churches in 144 countries. In 2006, membership in the United States was 353,995 in 1,875 churches.

"Dr. Walz offers his personal experience and insight, while entertaining and educating us, in a unique approach to achieving organizational and personal goals through the use of metaphors. By applying this cutting edge and innovative approach to your leadership, you will be assured to maintain the trajectory of your organization in a very complex and competitive marketplace."

—Kimberli Lewis, CEO

Global Business Therapy Europe &

President of European Database of Search and Publishing

With its headquarters located in Brussels, Belgium, and founded in 1966, the European Association of Directory Publishers (EADP) owes its existence to the aspirations of European publishers who anticipated the importance of intra-European contact and co-operation. Meanwhile, it has become the nerve center for year-round contact and the key representative for the industry. It is the only international association in Europe to speak for the sector as a whole. Today, the EADP has some 180 members in 36 countries world-wide, including member companies based in the 27 EU member states but also in the candidate countries: publishers, suppliers of products and services for the publishing industry and 5 national associations representing 340 directory publishers.

"I admit it—I'm a 'visual' kind of guy. Like many people, I understand abstract ideas much quicker when I am able to construct a mental picture of them. Metaphors are highly effective tools for painting such visual images, which makes them invaluable in communicating. Many of us, however, lack a systematic understanding of how and when to use metaphors. Jim Walz's new book provides great insights here, especially in application to the special challenges of business communication."

—Robert N. Mottice
President
Mottice Associates LLC

Throughout the world there are individuals who work to improve the lives of their countrymen through humanitarian efforts. These men and women provide services, create jobs, and provide hope in the midst of limited opportunities. Mottice Associates identifies these entrepreneurs and leverages their work through strategic planning, marketing, and finance. Their goal is to enable them to expand the breadth and scope of their activities and enlarge the population they serve. Their current efforts focus on Africa, Eastern Europe, and Latin America.

"There is no doubt that more and more I have come to appreciate and realize the importance and power of words and metaphors. This book must be a first to demonstrate with passion and effectiveness in Business and Leadership practices how to understand and make use of this important tool of language. The character of Jim Walz is shown in his artistic and creative style that makes for enjoyable reading. This book is timely and can only add value."

—Dr Michael Louis
Chairman – Cornerstone Institute
Chairman – Louis Group
Chairman: Hotels, Vineyards & Strategic Initiatives

With almost 100 years in business and its extensive financial and time investment in corporate social activities, The Louis Group has its international headquarters in South Africa. Its achievements have been recognized in South Africa's Top National Companies. Over and above the recognition of its commercial achievement, the Group has also been featured in Best Companies to Work for in South Africa, which confirms that the "family feel" of the Group has a consistently positive impact on its employees. The Corporate Research Foundation also awarded the Chairman and CEO the No. 1 Executive Management Team (2008/2009) and in the same year the No. 1 Best Managed Company in the Real Estate Sector.

"*'The soul... never thinks without a picture'*—Aristotle. In an endearing and entrepreneurial style Jim Walz has painted a picture with this book that every practitioner in change management needs to read. Delightfully and creatively, Jim has given new tools to what, without doubt, is the number one task of ever leader—helping others understand, embrace and prosper in 'change'. Analytical models just don't get the job done and never have—but in an easy to read, informative and rich style Jim's practical, thought provoking understanding of the power of metaphors will provide motivation to leaders and offer organizations new ways to address their development and strategic planning."

—Dr. Daniel "Dan" Lucero Ph.D., (MBA)

Entrepreneur, Teacher, Public Speaker, Humanitarian and International Development Worker, President of Foursquare France and ICFG Regional Rep to Western Africa and the French-speaking nations of the world.

Notes

Introduction

1. Ulaby (2009).

Chapter 2

1. Habicht (2001).
2. Elliott (2012).
3. Vadatum (2010).
4. Lipton (2008).
5. Mlodinow (2012).
6. Doidge (2007).
7. Bartlett (1932), p. 68.
8. Doidge (2007).
9. Levitan (2006).
10. Puk (2012, January), pp. 3–18.
11. Bartlett (1932), p. 68.

Chapter 6

1. Falkenhainer, Forbus, and Gentner (1989), pp. 1–63.

Chapter 15

1. The Brand Genius Award is an annual recognition of the brightest minds in advertising by *AdWeek*, a weekly American advertising trade journal.

Chapter 16

1. Falkenhainer, Forbus, and Gentner (1989), pp. 1–63.
2. Kuehne, Forbus, Gentner, and Quinn (2000, August), pp. 770–775.

References

Bartlett, F. C. (1932). *Remembering: A Study in experimental and social psychology* (p. 68). Cambridge, UK: Cambridge University Press.

Doidge, N. (2007). *The brain that changes Itself.* New York, NY: Penguin Books.

Elliott, R. (2012). *The secrets from our subconscious mind.* Bloomington, IN: iUniverse.

Falkenhainer, B., Forbus, K. D., & Gentner, D. (1989). The structure-mapping engine: Algorithm and examples. *Artificial Intelligence 41*(1), 1–63.

Habicht, M. (2001). *The mind and the unconscious—A modification of Freud's agencies.* Unpublished manuscript, Deakin University, Geelong, Australia.

Kuehne, S., Forbus, K., Gentner, D., & Quinn, B. (2000, August). *SEQL: Category learning as progressive abstraction using structure mapping* (pp. 770–775). In Proceedings of the 22nd Annual Meeting of the Cognitive Science Society.

Levitan, D. (2006). *This is your brain on music: The science of a human obsession.* New York, NY: Plume, Penguin Books.

Lipton, B. (2008). *The biology of belief: unleashing the power of consciousness, Matter, & Miracles.* New York, NY: Hayhouse, Inc.

Mlodinow, L. (2012). *Subliminal: How your unconscious mind rules your behavior.* New York, NY: Random House, Inc.

Puk, T. (2012). The influence of neurobiology on lifelong ecological literacy and ecological consciousness. *International Journal of Environmental & Science Education 7*(1), 3–18.

Ulaby, N. (2009). *And the death of tower records.* Retrieved April 14, 2013, from NPR Music: http://www.npr.org/2009/12/29/121975854/2006-and-the-death-of-tower-records

Vadatum, S. (2010). *The hidden brain: How our unconscious minds elect presidents, control markets, wage wars, and save our lives.* New York, NY: Random House, Inc.

Index

OTHER TITLES IN THE CORPORATE COMMUNICATION COLLECTION

Debbie DuFrene, Stephen F. Austin State University, Editor

- *Managing Investor Relations: Strategies for Effective Communication* by Alexander Laskin
- *Managing Virtual Teams* by Debbie DuFrene and Carol Lehman
- *Corporate Communication: Tactical Guidelines for Strategic Practice* by Michael Goodman and Peter B. Hirsch
- *Communication Strategies for Today's Managerial Leader* by Deborah Roebuck
- *Communication in Responsible Business: Strategies, Concepts, and Cases* by Roger N.Conaway and Oliver Laasch
- *Web Content: A Writer's Guide* by Janet Mizrahi
- *Intercultural Communication for Managers* by Michael B. Goodman
- *Today's Business Communication: A How-To Guide for the Modern Professional* by Jason L. Snyder and Robert Forbus
- *Fundamentals of Writing for Marketing and Public Relations: A Step-by-Step Guide for Quick and Effective Results* by Janet Mizrahi
- *Managerial Communication: Evaluating the Right Dose* by Johnson J. David

FORTHCOMING IN THIS COLLECTION

- *Communicating to Lead and Motivate 2/15/2014* by William C. Sharbrough
- *Leadership Talk A Discourse Approach to Leader Emergence 7/15/2014* by Robyn C. Walker and Yolanta Aritz
- *Communication Beyond Boundaries 8/15/2014* by Payal Mehra

Announcing the Business Expert Press Digital Library

Concise E-books Business Students Need
for Classroom and Research

This book can also be purchased in an e-book collection by your library as
- a one-time purchase,
- that is owned forever,
- allows for simultaneous readers,
- has no restrictions on printing, and
- can be downloaded as PDFs from within the library community.

Our digital library collections are a great solution to beat the rising cost of textbooks. e-books can be loaded into their course management systems or onto student's e-book readers.

The **Business Expert Press** digital libraries are very affordable, with no obligation to buy in future years. For more information, please visit **www.businessexpertpress.com/librarians**. To set up a trial in the United States, please contact **Adam Chesler** at *adam.chesler@ businessexpertpress.com* for all other regions, contact **Nicole Lee** at *nicole.lee@igroupnet.com*.

www.ingramcontent.com/pod-product-compliance
Lightning Source LLC
Chambersburg PA
CBHW050110210326
41519CB00015BA/3901